MW01641571
1939, 1943–1944 • Arthur French
1944–1967 • Nels Minné
1967–1977 • Robert DuFresne
1977–1983 • Robert Hanson
1983–1988 • Thomas Stark
1989–2005 • Darrell Krueger
2005–Present • Judith Ramaley
ersity Presidents

Her Star Shall Not Dim

A Sesquicentennial
History *of* Winona
State University

150 years
WINONA STATE
UNIVERSITY
1858 - 2008

Her Star Shall Not Dim

A Sesquicentennial History *of* Winona State University

Peter V. N. Henderson

WINONA
UNIVERSITY
18
58

Dedication

On behalf of the History Department, I would like to dedicate this book to the memories of Alex Yard and Zach Wilson.

THE
DONNING COMPANY
PUBLISHERS

The Donning Company Publishers
184 Business Park Drive, Suite 206
Virginia Beach, VA 23462-6533

Steve Mull, *Project Director*

Steve Mull, *General Manager*
Barbara B. Buchanan, *Office Manager*
Richard A. Horwege, *Senior Editor*
Mellanie Denny, *Graphic Designer*
Derek Eley, *Imaging Artist*
Cindy Smith, *Project Research Coordinator*
Scott Rule, *Director of Marketing*
Tonya Hannink, *Marketing Coordinator*

Library of Congress Cataloging-in-Publication Data

Henderson, Peter V. N., 1947–
Her star shall not dim : a sesquicentennial history of Winona State University / Peter V. N. Henderson.
p. cm.
Includes bibliographical references and index.
ISBN 978-1-57864-458-2 (hard cover : alk. paper)
1. Winona State University—History. I. Title.
LD6092.H46 2007
378.776'12—dc22

2007037409

Printed in the USA at Walsworth Publishing Company

WINONA STATE
UNIVERSITY
1858 - 2008

Table of Contents

Introduction

For those of you who are saying to yourself, "But I just put down a book about Winona State history," the author wishes to remind you of a longstanding maxim holding that universities need to rewrite their histories every twenty-five years. Certainly the arrival of the momentous Sesquicentennial Celebration is sufficient justification for a fresh look at our university's heritage. Like my predecessors, I will proceed largely chronologically. But unlike earlier versions of the story, this one will focus more heavily on recent events, those fresh in the minds of alumni, faculty, administrators, students, and friends of the university. Those interested in a more in-depth and factual account of the early days of Winona State, can turn to Clyde O. Ruggles's *Historical Sketch and Notes: Winona State Normal School, 1860–1910*. Lured away from Winona State by Harvard University, where he pursued a brilliant academic career, Ruggles had a particular bent for turn-of-phrase that the present author hopes to emulate. Hence, another goal of my volume is to make this institutional history enjoyable, not just for the selfish reason of hoping that many alums will purchase copies, but more importantly, so the story of Winona State's success will reach a broad audience.

To further the goal of appealing to the now nearly fifty thousand graduates of Winona State (some of whom admittedly have passed on to their just reward over the past 150 years), the many friends of the university from our city and across the state of Minnesota, and the community of Winona State faculty and administrators (both retired and still serving), the present volume will attempt to avoid some of the pitfalls facing institutional authors. Rather than focus entirely on the person of the president and his accomplishments, as many such histories tend to do, I will look at leadership as just one of the themes that have joined in weaving together Winona State's complex heritage. Students, faculty, and the citizens of Winona have each made outstanding contributions to the institutional success story, and researching yearbooks and student newspapers and watching the interviews collected by the WSU Retiree Center provided color for this story. Further, this narrative will be told within the context of the historical development of the state and of educational theory. Each of the four chapters will examine the following five themes that run throughout Winona State's history: the school's innovative role in the state and region; its leadership moving the institution forward (or not); its partnerships with the city of Winona and the state to further public policy; its commitment to a social contract viewing education as a public good to serve the state and region; and, finally, the evolution of quality and higher standards, in terms of both curriculum and the physical plant.

Winona State University has always prided itself in breaking new ground, especially within the state of Minnesota. From the moment that it emerged as the first teachers' college west of the Mississippi River (or as geography would have it in our case, south of the river), Winona became synonymous with innovations in education, whether as a proponent of newfangled theories of education in the 1880s and 1890s, the initiator of the kindergarten movement west of the Mississippi, the advocate for assessment of student learning, or the leading proponent of scholarly engagement with the community. Frequently, though not always, strong presidents propelled these ideas forward, ably assisted by faculty and administrators convinced of the wisdom of these innovations. Strong leadership also enabled the institution to weather the various crises that confronted it and at times threatened Winona State's very existence.

A third constant, which began in the 1850s, was the institution's partnership with the city of Winona, whose civic leaders saw the value of an institution of higher learning, lobbied hard for its creation, and offered their private funds to advance Winona State. Community generosity remains high in the twenty-first century as evidenced in the outpouring of support for the university's building projects and its quality initiatives in tough economic times.

Fourth, from the time that Minnesota became a territory in the 1840s until the present in which it received the sobriquet of "the brain state," policymakers have seen the value of public education as a public good. Along with the lawman and the farmer, the schoolmarm tamed the frontier and brought civilization to the West. More recently, education has played a vital role in training a highly qualified professional work force that has helped to give Minnesota a balanced and viable economy. As time has passed, Winona State's social contract (an unwritten but omnipresent ethical ideal) with the state has led to the education of captains of industry, public figures, and ordinary good citizens who vote and pay taxes. Finally, over the past 150 years, Winona State has advanced from an institution that essentially offered a two-year teaching certificate program to a full-blown university that offers undergraduate and graduate degrees in select programs. From a borrowed four-room schoolhouse in downtown Winona, it has evolved into an aesthetically pleasing campus with up-to-date facilities.

(To be fair though, blackboards were as technologically advanced in the 1860s because they made knowledge visible as LCD projectors and laptop computers are today.)

In writing a history of this sort I have naturally incurred significant intellectual debts, and this provides me with an opportunity to thank all those individuals who assisted with the project. First, I thank Presidents Darrell Krueger and Judith Ramaley and the members of the administrative team for the financial assistance necessary to complete the project. Congressman Tim Penny, chair of the Sesquicentennial Committee, and all the members of the committee, especially Vice President Jim Schmidt, helped to make this project possible. I want to give special thanks to Marianna Byman, Wayne Dunbar, Fred Foss, Rod Henry, Mark Peterson, Judith Ramaley, Jim Reynolds, David Robinson, and Greg Schmidt, each of whom read the entire rough draft, corrected errors, and added valuable material to the final version. Nine extra pairs of eyes really help. They are not responsible, however, for any errors I inserted thereafter. In addition, I would like to thank Joe Emanuel, Jim Reynolds, Wayne Erickson, Judy Schlawin, Fred Foss, and Dan Hoyt for participating in a "round-table" to share their reminiscences about the university's recent past. Jim Reineke provided very useful information about the recent history of education. Thanks also to Shirley Wheat and Lisa Hessel, who transformed my chicken scratching into real English language words. To the many alumni, faculty, administrators, emeriti, and students who helped to build this great institution, the entire Sesquicentennial Committee is most grateful. Finally, I would like to thank my colleagues in the History Department, past and present, for their friendship and support during my time at Winona State. I hope that the above, and many more, will enjoy this labor of love.

The First Teachers' College West of the Mississippi

Chapter 1

In the autumn of 1851, Captain Orrin B. Smith and a group of would-be pioneers, anticipating the ratification of the Treaty of Mendota that allowed white settlement in Minnesota, steamed their way north along the Mississippi River on what is today the border between Minnesota and Wisconsin. The beauty of the natural surroundings stunned the small group of men hardened by collective years of experience in the middle part of the United States. The volume of water descending the river made the steamboat's paddles strain, forcing them to keep away from the main current and inadvertently appreciate the splendid natural setting. Six-hundred-foot-high bluffs girded the river, marking its ten-million-year course. From river's edge to the farthest vista, tall hardwoods crowded the landscape, lending a moist, verdant hue to the soft autumn day. Aesthetics, however, mattered little to the new pioneers. Stirred by a restless, ambitious spirit to conquer a new land and make a home for their families, they viewed the rich Minnesota territory and particularly the endless forests as a place where they could carve out a better future than they had previously imagined possible.

Choosing a suitable settlement location proved easy. For a number of years Captain Smith had eyed the place now known as Winona, a long and narrow flat sandbar, once an island in the mighty river that now formed the south shore. Like previous travelers, he appreciated Winona's favorable location. No doubt French fur trappers plying their trade among the Native Americans of the region had put in and camped at Winona. Certainly the Native Americans esteemed the location, still used in 1851 as a summer residence by Chief Wapasha and his band of Lakota Sioux. According to legend, Winona received its name from Wapasha's first-born daughter, who, when thwarted in her choice of husbands by her father's strong will, threw herself from the top of Garvin Heights rather than accept the unwanted suitor. (Similar legends sprinkle Native American communities throughout the Midwest.) Smith's settlers bought off Wapasha who relinquished his claims to Winona in exchange for "inviolable rights" further west in Minnesota where no white men would ever want to venture, and the families and inevitable land speculators took possession.

Although it was getting late in the season, Smith's band of pioneers chopped trees and hurriedly built shelters, knowing winter was on the way. What they did not realize was that the several hundred miles they had journeyed north from St. Louis would make such a difference in climate. Wintry blasts shook the walls of the little cabins early in November, and soon the river froze, cutting off communication and supplies from the south. But the hearty pioneers could trade for food with a few friendly Native Americans in the vicinity, and the frozen river still provided fish once a hearty soul augured a hole through the ice. The settlers persevered, and as winter finally turned to spring, they began to think about ways that they could earn a living. Newcomers and their families usually hoped to carve out a small farm, others of greater vision looked to the vast forests as a source of wealth. With hundreds of thousands of immigrants pouring into the Midwest and cities sprouting from the plains, people needed building materials, which in the nineteenth century meant lumber. A few settlers began buying up large tracts of land at very reasonable prices and employing others as loggers.

In fact, logging and farming proved to be symbiotic experiences, because a man could tend his fields in the summer and then head off to a lumber camp in winter (while his family huddled for warmth in one of the poorly lit, drafty, uninsulated homes of Winona). The newly founded community soon became the center of the local lumber industry. As early as 1855, several of the most successful lumber barons opened sawmills that employed hundreds of newcomers to the settlement. During the winter the men trekked farther and farther into the north woods on the Wisconsin side of the river seeking pine, oak, and other native species. The process of lumbering adapted to the climate. Teams of horses pulled huge felled and de-limbed trees along ice roads to a river bank. In the spring, when streams like the Chippewa River thawed and flooded into the Mississippi, loggers rode the log rafts downstream to the mills. These logging drives continued until 1915. By then, deforestation had destroyed the industry's economic viability. As a lumber town, Winona prospered, quickly sustaining a population of about twenty thousand within a few decades of the city's founding.

Prosperity and the search for wealth alone did not call the pioneers into southeastern Minnesota. Unlike the Spanish conquistadors who pillaged for loot in sixteenth-century Latin America and settled the land as a by-product of their greed, Minnesota pioneers usually brought their families to their new homes. Most of these settlers had spent time in the eastern part of the United States and knew that the American ethos evoked the idea of opportunity for the common man. As part of that opportunity, pioneers inherently understood that education represented a positive good, and the settlers of Minnesota provided generously for education in the territorial constitution, where fully one-eighteenth of the territory's land (a figure chosen because there are 640 acres in a section) was set aside for educational purposes. Obviously, this did not mean that all that land would be occupied by school buildings, but rather that the state could sell or lease such property to help subsidize the cost of education. By 1857, leading lights of the Winona community like Dr. John Ford had begun to advocate for public education, particularly the innovative notion of the "normal school" as a method of satisfying the desire of a frontier community to bring civilization to its midst.

A trained physician, Ford had left his native Connecticut for health reasons, thinking that battling the rigors of the Minnesota climate might reinvigorate him. By facing physical adversity one could overcome disease, or so the thinking of the time went. (Such notions would send the puny, asthmatic Theodore Roosevelt to North Dakota a few years later, where he became both exemplar and proponent of the strenuous life through physical exertion.) Dr. Ford's experiences proved to be similar on a smaller scale, for he regained his health for a decade and, more importantly, became the leading proponent of the normal school movement in the state. Reduced to its simplest terms, the idea of the normal school was to prepare prospective teachers in the methods of instruction that maximized student learning. In the nineteenth century the normal school movement sought specifically to certify qualified teachers for elementary schools. To give elementary-age students adequate "book learning" to enable them to function in the business world and become good citizens, these early elementary schools focused on imparting the three Rs (reading, 'riting, and 'rithmetic). Proponents of the normal school movement believed that their graduates were adequately equipped to teach young minds these essential subjects and values.

Tracing its origins back to the innovative methodology of the famous French Christian Brothers school in the 1680s, the normal school movement progressed to Germany and Great Britain where it took root and blossomed. Prominent American educators like Horace Mann traveled to Great Britain in the 1820s to study the movement and bring relevant ideas back to Massachusetts. There the first normal school was founded at Framingham, and others sprouted not only elsewhere in that state but shortly thereafter in Connecticut, New York, and New Jersey. Hence, it is not surprising that a Connecticut native, John Ford, would know about the movement and be a proponent of the innovation. Starting in the mid-1850s, Ford began to campaign for the concept in Winona. Rallying support proved quite easy in the progressive river community. Newspapers like the *Winona Republican* heralded the idea of a normal school as an institution that would provide great benefits to the state as well as the local community. Championing the idea at the state legislature was one of Winona's great attorneys and later US senator, Daniel S. Norton. The foresightedness of Winona's civic leadership should not be underestimated. No other state west of the great river had developed innovative public policy about education, and many states to the south and east also lagged far behind. Merely conceptualizing the idea, however, did not make the dream a reality, and now Ford and Norton took on the job of pragmatic politicians, lobbying for legislative support.

Even a decade after Minnesota became a territory in 1849, the state's legislature typified the rough and tumble of frontier politics. Nattily dressed lawyers and businessmen, largely from the capital of St. Paul and its twin sister, the growing city of Minneapolis, dueled for attention with rough-hewn farmers clad in overalls. All, however, shared a love of tobacco: the floor of the chamber glittered with brass spittoons, and cigar smoke filled the room. The hurley-burley of the politicians and their friends resembled a county fair. Yet in spite of the confusion, the smoke, and the demagoguery, the legislature managed to conduct important business. Certainly a vast majority of the members shared a concern for the public good and took very seriously their task of carving out a better society on the frontier than the one that they had known elsewhere. Hence, it is not surprising that the innovative notion of creating normal schools met with nearly universal approval during the session in 1858.

In those days the legislature met during the summer, a convenient time for farmers, whose crops were already in the ground, and for lawyers and businessmen, whose activities tapered off somewhat in the hot and humid months. The absence of snow and ice facilitated attendance in St. Paul and allowed for the conduct of effective sessions. Because of his driving interest in the concept of the normal school, Dr. Ford attended the 1858 session and even drafted a bill, proposing that a normal school be founded at Winona. Ford's reputation as an educational innovator lent him great credibility at the legislature. Already he had persuaded the elementary school in Winona to adopt the "graded" system, where students were ranked according to the levels of learning they had achieved, then passed from grade to grade after mastering the next level of knowledge. The idea of the graded one-room schoolhouse was at the cutting edge of educational theory in the 1850s: Winona's graded school was the first in the state. Yet Ford's reputation as an innovator and Senator Norton's political influence proved inadequate to pass the legislation as drafted. "Favoritism," its opponents cried. And so the legislature crafted a compromise bill that created a farsighted normal school system for all of Minnesota.

To further education in the state, the legislature redrew the map of Minnesota to create three normal school districts that reflected the distribution of the state's population in the 1850s and roughly approximated the state's judicial districts. The first district took in southeastern Minnesota, stretching from the Mississippi River westward for a hundred miles and north almost to St. Paul. A second district included Mankato and southwestern Minnesota, while the third district included the small town of St. Cloud and the remainder of the state north and west. Creating thus a sense of a "service region," the legislature provided for the long-term development of a normal school system in the state. But it did not envision the normal school system as an entirely state-funded, state-controlled enterprise. Rather, it counted on considerable regional influence by requiring that local representatives comprise the membership of the State Normal School Board, without going to the extreme measure of creating a board for each campus. Even more importantly, the legislature agreed to charter and fund the first of the three districts that raised $5,000 for the purpose of creating a normal school (an early version of a matching grant, in a sense). Minnesota's governor, Henry H. Sibley, signed the legislation that created the normal school system in 1858. In getting more than he originally sought, Dr. Ford rightly earned his designation as the "father of the normal school system in Minnesota."

The indefatigable Dr. Ford brought news of the legislative triumph home to Winona and turned immediately to his well-heeled friends in the community in meeting the legislature's challenge. His unassailable reputation as an educational leader was complemented by his valuable role as frontier physician. Mysterious diseases and frequently inexplicable deaths from epidemics made doctors a valuable commodity for nineteenth-century communities, even though medical science remained inexact at the time. The much-respected Dr. Ford managed to raise the required $5,000 in a matter of hours, according to legend. Indeed, the original contributors donated an extra $2,000 in cash and land. Not only the wealthy but even those of lesser means contributed. Today, of course, $7,000 seems like a modest amount to raise, well within the reach of even working-class families. In the 1850s, however, the situation was much different. Few individuals enjoyed access to much hard cash in the first place. Farmers often bartered for goods they needed, and even tradesmen in downtown Winona took goods in lieu of coins. Second, the dollar enjoyed much higher value in the 1850s. A worker in a lumber mill would earn about $300 a year at best, and the average family farm owner even less. Hence,

$5,000 in cash represented a huge sum of money, perhaps equivalent to $150,000 in today's dollars.

With the donations from the community secured, Dr. Ford pressed the State Normal School Board to establish the state's first normal school at Winona, which it agreed to do in 1859. But the community's generosity had not yet been exhausted. The city agreed to donate for a period of eight years a small building wherein the normal school could begin to offer classes, starting in September 1860. From the time of the creation of the institution (and arguably even before), the importance of the city of Winona to the fledgling normal school was undeniable. Even in these early years, community leaders understood the value of supporting the normal school for the betterment of the community and the state as a whole. But if the school were to open in 1860, Ford and the other community leaders had much to do in the interim. Specifically, they had to locate a president (called the principal in those days), hire a faculty, set up a curriculum, and recruit students for the fall class.

In 1858 the residents of Winona raised enough money to meet the Minnesota legislature's criteria for selection as the site for the state's first normal school. Winona Normal trained teachers who taught in frontier schools. A year later the city donated the first classroom building for the school that would one day become Winona State University. The initial enrollment was twenty students.

Seeking a suitable principal was Dr. Ford's first responsibility, and he chose John Ogden, an experienced normal school advocate from Ohio. Tall and strapping, with a commanding presence, Ogden had begun his professional life as a blacksmith, a very important role in frontier communities. After being kicked by a horse and gravely injured, Ogden opted for a safer occupation and soon found he had a natural bent for teaching. Years of on-the-job experience rather than impressive academic credentials prepared him for the principalship at Winona. Besides, Ogden shared the teaching with William Stearns, who had graduated from Harvard University, and a local doctor, David Reid, who lectured about chemistry. At the opening of the Winona Normal School in September of 1860, Principal Ogden delivered a stirring speech in which he told the assembled group of students and community members that the purpose of the normal school was not just to provide an education but to encourage, "the development of the whole character of the individual, physically, educationally, morally, and religiously." Predicting a bright future for Winona State, he concluded, "her star shall not dim." Winona Normal opened its doors for formal instruction with a class of twenty students, mostly female.

Measured by today's standards, admissions requirements were not very rigorous. Pupils needed to be at least sixteen years old and of good moral character. They were not required to be high school graduates (in fact that was very rare in these early years), but to pass a basic entrance examination that tested their abilities in English, mathematics, and geography. Much as was the case with the military academies, students needed to be nominated by state senators. Further, they paid no tuition, instead pledging to teach for at least two years somewhere in the state of Minnesota upon completing the course of study. The three-year program began with a solely remedial year in the three Rs, while the next two years of work required some higher level courses and several courses in educational methods. At each year's end, based on a tradition dating back to medieval Europe, students underwent public oral examinations where they exposed their learning (or lack thereof) to the public at large.

The initial enrollment of twenty was higher than expected, but such was the thirst for learning and employment as teachers in the young state. Clara Caswell, a graduate of one of the first classes, left her impression of traveling for the first time to Winona Normal in the 1860s. No railroad had come to Winona yet, and only a few students took the steamboats that now regularly plied the Mississippi River. Travel by stagecoach cost dearly, and so most students arrived in Winona on the seat of the family buckboard. As she bumped along the narrow Burns Valley road, the prospect of passing another wagon and being shoved off the very narrow path frightened Miss Caswell. So, too, did the size of Winona. For many farm girls, a city that held three thousand people in the 1860s was daunting by itself. Then came the prospect of boarding with strangers, because not every student had a relative in Winona with whom she could live, and no dormitories existed in this world. As in the beloved story of Laura Ingalls Wilder in *Little House on the Prairie*, a school like Winona Normal offered a unique opportunity for a young woman who would otherwise be consigned to the life of a farm wife or a laborer in a factory. Finding employment as a town's schoolmarm offered a rewarding and challenging future of public service, adventure, and freedom otherwise not available to nineteenth-century women.

Even as the hardy young women and men enrolled at Winona completed their oral examinations at the end of their first year, cannon shells rocked the federal emplacements at Fort Sumter, South Carolina, and the Civil War began. As Southern states seceded one after another, and the United States appeared to be on the verge of disintegrating, President Abraham Lincoln called for volunteers to preserve the Union. Viewing the flags in the rotunda at the state capitol building in St. Paul, one can certainly conclude that Minnesota contributed its fair share of volunteer regiments to the cause. In fact, on a per capita basis Minnesota sent more men to the ensuing war than any other Northern state. A strong principled leader like John Ogden felt he had no choice but to serve, so in the fall of 1861 he announced that he had joined a Wisconsin regiment as a captain. Ogden fought well in the war, but was captured while recruiting an African-American regiment in Tennessee and held as a prisoner of war for nearly a year. From all accounts, being a POW in a Southern camp was extremely harsh, but Ogden survived the experience and after the war returned to the field of education if not to Winona, serving most notably as the president of Fisk University in Nashville. (He was vibrantly alive in 1910 when Winona Normal celebrated its fifty-year anniversary.) After Ogden left in 1861, William Stearns also enlisted, as did most of the male members of the college. Following the abbreviated winter term in 1861, the State Normal School Board decided to close the school temporarily.

As was the case for many of the men fighting in the Civil War, the wound to the school was serious but not fatal. The principles that underpinned the founding of Winona Normal still held true. The citizens of the community, and particularly Dr. John Ford, believed that the mission of the school was too important to surrender. It had already carved out a place by being the first institution of its kind west of the Mississippi. The people of Minnesota, whether defined as the members of the legislature or the parents who sent their sons or daughters to Winona, had endorsed the idea of a public institution whose students were dedicated to improving their world. Consequently, as the war began to wind down in 1864, with the prospects of a Northern victory more and more inevitable, Dr. Ford and his friends in the Winona community began to plan for the reopening of the normal school.

The Idea of the Model School

The end of the Civil War ushered in a new era throughout America. If the South saw revolutionary change at least for a while, the North underwent its own evolutionary rebuilding process. In southeastern Minnesota the economy diversified, adding rippling waves of cornfields to the majestic greenery and small farms that had once lined the river. As with real estate today, location was everything, and Winona's placement on a relatively calm shore of the great river made it an ideal port of embarkation for the grains produced in the hinterland. After a small sputter, the Winona economy reconstructed itself, and the city remained prosperous. Likewise, the normal school survived the test of the Civil War, reopening even before the war's end in the fall of 1864.

Rendering his last great service to Winona Normal, Dr. Ford undertook to find a new principal to replace John Ogden. Not content to hire just anyone who could perform the duties, Ford wanted the new principal to be a real innovator, someone on the cutting edge of the latest normal school philosophies. Nor was he willing to let applications just drift in for the job. Instead, he boarded a train for the East Coast to seek out someone connected to what would later be described as the Oswego Movement, after the normal school founded in 1861 in Oswego, New York. After talking to knowledgeable people, Ford narrowed his search to William Phelps, a renowned figure in American education and at that moment the principal of one of New Jersey's normal schools, in Trenton. By fortunate coincidence, Phelps, remembered by his contemporaries as a homely, angular man but one of high principles, was anxious to leave Trenton and be free of his "old fogy board." Interviewing Phelps at his campus, Ford was highly impressed and offered him the job. The two shared many ideas, and Phelps jumped at the opportunity to have a free hand to innovate. Not long after Phelps took office, however, Ford fell victim to one of his recurring asthmatic spells, which this time resulted in his death. Nevertheless, Ford's lasting influence was such that the State Normal School Board endorsed all of the ideas that Phelps introduced into the curriculum, as well as the new faculty he hired, most of whom had been trained at Oswego.

As an educational theory, the Oswego Movement took its ideas from reforms conceptualized by the Swiss educator Johann Heinrich Pestalozzi earlier in the century and subsequently modified by a series of British theoreticians. Referred to commonly as the Pestalozzian reforms or sometimes as "object teaching," the ideas of the Oswego Movement laid the foundation for modern elementary education. To oversimplify, the Oswego Movement believed in two essential principles. First, children's learning followed a natural order of development, which roughly corresponded with age, but did differ from individual to individual. Growing maturity, then, affected how children learned as well as the type of material that they were capable of understanding. (This first principle fit well with Ford's older notion of a graded school.) Second, the Oswego Movement emphasized the importance of concrete experiences that would develop knowledge and inspire curiosity to learn more (action precedes reflection). But the mere acquisition of knowledge was deemed insufficient. The Oswego school believed its ultimate aim was "fitness for life . . . and preparation for individual action." In other words, graduates of elementary schools needed more than the three Rs; they needed to understand the importance of promoting societal welfare and needed to have the courage and skill to advance the public good.

Perhaps the best-known summation of Phelps's philosophy was the belief that "education has to work on the hand, the head, and the heart" (also referred to as the three Hs). By exposing the young child to the natural world's wonders, a good teacher would pique the pupil's curiosity. Perception of natural objects would lead, as the child matured, to a conception of more abstract ideas. Ultimately, the sophisticated older student would be able to make comparisons, relate ideas, discover cause-and-effect relationships, and finally, undertake analysis. Coupled with this knowledge would come a sense of responsibility toward the community and a self-induced desire to promote the general good. To inspire young teachers with such deeply held beliefs would in turn, Phelps believed, promote the public good. And so this ideologically motivated educational reformer came to Winona to make his mark. With him, Phelps also brought the idea of the "model school," originally a school for pupils aged six to twelve, run by the normal school, for which Winona and other normal schools would become famous.

The new educational philosophy required a new second- and third-year curriculum that Phelps quickly put into place. The first-year curriculum focused on the "common branches," a remedial basic studies program that high school graduates would ordinarily have completed. The second-year curriculum instructed students in what today we would describe as the professional education sequence, where prospective teachers learned the

Normal school principal William Phelps, a pioneer in the "model school" movement, established one in Winona shortly after the Civil War. As an extension of Winona Normal School, the model school offered future teachers a laboratory school and gave the community a cutting-edge elementary and secondary educational facility. These kindergarten children are pictured in Ogden Hall, circa 1910.

essence of the Pestalozzian system. In the third year, advanced students spent most of their time working with the model school. Citizens of the community paid a modest tuition for their children to attend the school, where Phelps and his staff did much of the instruction. In part, the advanced students learned by observing and working with master teachers, among them Miss Mary Lee, considered by students the best instructor of the Phelps era. Beyond that, they had the opportunity to practice-teach. A few in each class washed out at this critical juncture, finding themselves inadequate for the job or being found so by the faculty and subsequently dismissed. Phelps and the faculty thus hoped that Winona Normal would continue to offer a two-year teaching degree (once the year of remedial work had been completed), but a degree ideally imbued with the more challenging Pestalozzian philosophy. Although the first class faltered and nobody graduated in 1865 (a student not only had to pass the examinations, but also be free from "character defects"), eventually Winona's first graduating class passed through commencement exercises in the spring of 1866 following three full days of oral examinations open to the public. In addition, the children of the model school performed to

Winona Normal School's first permanent building, "Old Main," opened in 1868. This state-of-the-art facility contained natural science artifacts and an art gallery. Eager to help the school succeed, Winona residents donated objects and money for the collections it contained.

the satisfaction of the entire community, thus demonstrating the effectiveness of Pestalozzian pedagogy.

Whether because of or despite the changing administration and the reformed academic program, students continued to enroll at Winona Normal in record numbers. More and more settlers had entered Minnesota, and European immigrants began to make their mark. Swedes, Norwegians, and Germans flocked to the state, bringing customs and foods (like lutefisk) to diversify the life of the region. The number of farms rapidly increased. Growing towns dotted the landscape, as ethnic groups tried to recreate the communities they had left behind. These immigrants also believed in the civilizing power of education, so the demand for schoolteachers multiplied. As record numbers of students crowded into the small four-room wooden structure at the corner of Fourth and Lafayette that the city had generously provided, Phelps recognized the need for something more permanent if Winona Normal was to continue to grow and serve the interests of the region. Hence, he decided to ask the legislature to fund the construction of a building that would be sufficiently large to house all of the elements of a normal school based on Pestalozzian principles: classrooms, a library room, a museum (used to help teach geography), the model school, and an art gallery (also for pedagogical purposes).

Creating a physical plant lent a permanency to the normal school that otherwise might not have existed. When the state had committed to a campus, it gave the normal school a plot of land at Block 17 of the Sanborn Division (now located near the Amtrak Station). Community leader Henry Huff, a real estate speculator, newspaperman, and hotel owner, argued that the normal school ought to be located in a central part of the city closer to the river and not relegated to the outskirts of the community. So he agreed to donate a more valuable parcel he owned at Block 4 of the Sanborn Division as the site of the school. Once again, the generous philanthropy of a community member who believed in the value of the normal school's work proved essential. Unlike some of Winona's sister institutions, granted huge parcels of land outside city environs, Winona's campus has from the first been integrally tied to the community, usually for the benefit of both. When the normal school needed to expand physically, the state purchased nearby properties that have enabled the campus to grow to its present dimensions.

Principal Phelps hired an architect and worked closely with him on the building that became known as Old Main. Over two sessions the legislature appropriated $50,000 for the construction of the three-story building. Equally importantly, the city of Winona, or rather generous residents, nearly matched the state contribution, thereby helping to make Phelps' dream a reality. As it has so often done, the community demonstrated its farsighted commitment to the normal school project. As Senator E. S. Youmans stated in advocating for the permanent structure, "This state must have a Normal School . . . it is entirely indispensable." With various dignitaries present, including Lieutenant Governor Ignatius Donnelly, a nationally known figure in the labor movement, Phelps laid the cornerstone in 1866 with a time capsule of documents buried beneath it. By 1868 a grand brick structure met the eyes of students who had traveled from as far away as Ramsey County to enroll. With its neo-Gothic features, airy classrooms, and model school, Old Main was a state-of-the-art facility, consistent architecturally with a number of other normal schools around the country. In keeping with Pestalozzian philosophy, Phelps organized a museum of minerals, fossils, and other natural specimens from the region (much like the collection currently in Pasteur Hall) so that model school students could actually handle the artifacts that they were studying. Many of the objects in the museum and the art gallery resulted from donations of objects or money by citizens of Winona eager again to contribute to the success of the Winona Normal School. Further, the college sent its science instructor, John Holzinger, east so that he could learn the latest techniques of museum metholology for organizing the collection. By the time America's centennial rolled around in 1876, Winona Normal had in many respects reached the apogee of Phelps's principalship, with the new building fully occupied and with faculty trained in the most innovative educational philosophy delivering the content of the courses.

But as so often the best of times were also the worst of times. Reeling from economic depression and the scandals associated with President Ulysses S. Grant, the United States was scarcely in the mood to celebrate the hundredth anniversary of independence in the exuberant manner that it deserved. Likewise, the Minnesota legislature glumly looked at its revenues (the ability to tax was much more limited in the nineteenth century) and decided to make no appropriation to the three normal schools at Winona, Mankato, and St. Cloud. Critics argued that normal schools represented local rather than state interests; a number of students had reneged on their pledge to teach for two years and allegedly many who attended the free school could well afford tuition at a private college. Other legislators thought that the money could be better spent elsewhere. Phelps, who had quarreled with his board in New Jersey and left Trenton because of the lack of support he felt there, promptly resigned in protest and took a position at what is today the University of Wisconsin–Whitewater, then a fledgling normal school. Not content there, he soon resigned and retired back to Winona, where he spent the remainder of his life, until 1907, serving as the superintendent of Winona's public schools and publishing articles about education.

The state legislature's failure to appropriate funds sent the State Normal School Board into a frenzy. Some voices shouted for the institutions to close, probably the outcome desired by a number of the passive-aggressive legislators who did not want to face angry voters by acting directly to close the schools. By all reports, Winona's representative to the State Normal School Board led the fight to keep the institutions functioning. Ironically, previous legislative acts hampered Winona Normal's ability to react to its second great crisis. By denying the institutions the right to request assistance from local contributors, the legislature had handicapped the ability of Winona Normal to meet the fiscal challenge. In fact, several city benefactors, on hearing of the legislature's failure to appropriate, had approached the institution with an offer to pay all operating expenses, but were told such gifts could no longer be accepted.

Keeping the institution running would call for creative fundraising, and finally the State Normal School Board devised a method that worked and fit state guidelines. The school had long charged tuition to local high school students enrolled in the first of the three years offered. (Finishing the first year at the normal school granted the equivalent of a high school diploma.) In addition, the normal school had educated free of charge a large number of Civil War orphans who lived anywhere in the state, as well as the elementary students enrolled at the model school who paid a modest tuition. Winona Normal's new principal, Charles A. Morey, took the bold step of increasing tuition to meet the shortfall. Community leaders contributed as well, agreeing to pay tuition for the orphans who previously had attended free of charge. Morey also reduced expenses. Faculty and staff tightened their belts and took a pay cut, and a number of faculty lost their jobs. As a result, Winona Normal struggled through the academic year (as did Mankato and St. Cloud). At its next session the rather embarrassed state legislature restored funding to the normal schools and made that funding a permanent base so that a crisis year like 1876 would never again threaten the schools' existence.

Winona Normal in the Gilded Age, 1876–1904

The last quarter of the nineteenth century, nicknamed the Gilded Age (a term coined by Mark Twain), represented in popular literature an era of greed and excess, exploitation and poverty. Underneath the tales of the extremes, however, lay the less dramatic but more important expansion of the middle class. Although Minnesota had its share of plutocrats—as very rich men like James J. Hill of St. Paul who owned the Great Northern Railroad were called—the wealth of the state generally was shared. Cities like Minneapolis and St. Paul mushroomed, dwarfing earlier rivals like Winona, whose population remained modestly near twenty thousand. Immigrants, many of whom arrived poor but were willing to work hard to achieve economic success, shared many of the same goals as the old-timers, and particularly desired universal public education for their children. Demographic statistics pointed out the need for additional teachers, and Winona Normal's enrollments reflected that demand. Bolstered by these public policy arguments, Winona's leaders, both at the normal school and within the community, were committed to providing a quality education, and in turn increasingly demanded better prepared new-entering students. As a result, the institution made modest gains and held its reputation as an innovative normal school. The city's thirst for higher education also resulted in the founding of two private Catholic schools, St. Mary's and St. Theresa's, early in the twentieth century.

In the midst of the crisis of 1876, Winona Normal had found a capable replacement for Phelps from among its own faculty. Given the imminent crisis, the State Normal School Board decided it had no time to conduct a leisurely search as had Dr. Ford a decade before. A gruff disciplinarian with a caustic wit, Charles Morey seems to have been the right person for that critical situation. Finishing at the head of his class in 1872 at Winona Normal, Morey had been given a modest scholarship to continue his education towards a BA at the Massachusetts Institute of Technology, today one of the best science and math institutions in the country and in the 1870s a path-breaking educational institution intended to be relevant to the new industrial America. Winona Normal funded Morey's further education on the condition that he return to the school and take a position on the faculty to teach physics, chemistry, and the manual arts. Although at twenty-five, Morey was very young for a principal, Winona knew his strengths and foibles well, and he provided two important new directions for the school.

Upon his return to Winona as a faculty member, Morey set up the institution's first science laboratories, where he instructed students in physics and chemistry. Laboratory sciences had an intensely pragmatic purpose in the Gilded Age, for after all, this was the era of Thomas Edison and Alexander Graham Bell. Across the country new technology greatly altered the American way of life, whether in the home or at work. Hence, the laboratory sciences included the "manual arts," or industrial arts as the program later came to be named. Winona's professors had to be equipped to instruct teachers who would in turn be molding the scientific minds of the future. Morey himself loved to tinker, having worked briefly as an apprentice with Alexander Graham Bell, so it is not surprising that the demanding young president would want to see the sciences well represented at Winona Normal. In fact, Morey was the first of three presidents in Winona State's history with a scientific background—the others being Nels Minné and the current president Judith A. Ramaley—and for that the college owes him a debt for his efforts championing science. As the normal school began training secondary teachers, the role of laboratory sciences took on an increased importance.

Morey's second reform was to toughen standards, because requirements for entering Winona Normal and becoming a teacher were less than rigorous by modern expectations. He and the faculty wanted to change the traditional pattern of education in the state, which saw the vast majority of enrollees completing their high school work at the normal institution before beginning the education sequence or taking the education classes and earning a high school diploma elsewhere later. (In these early years, one theoretically only needed an eighth-grade education to be eligible to teach.) Forcing the remedial students to pay tuition, Morey believed, would tilt the scales in favor of high school graduates, although a generation later the old pattern still persisted. "Toughen the entrance standards," Morey and the faculty shouted, and the State Normal School Board agreed. To ensure the state that Winona Normal students were well prepared, Morey began the practice of issuing end-of-term grade reports. Both tougher admission criteria and expelling nonperforming students had the effect of reducing enrollment temporarily, but soon the more rigorous curriculum and more valuable degree attracted better students to the college. By the time Morey resigned the presidency in 1879 to practice law, the enrollment had returned to more typical numbers.

Nevertheless, Morey remained the *eminence grise* (power behind the throne) for many years at Winona Normal, serving as the school's representative to the State Normal School Board well into the twentieth century. He also achieved prominence as the president of Winona National Bank (after William Windom, who moved on to the US Senate and eventually became secretary of the treasury under Presidents James Garfield and Benjamin Harrison). Imagine the next president's discomfiture at having his two immediate predecessors, Phelps and Morey, in prominent positions in the community, looking over his shoulder at every decision. On the other hand, because Irwin Shepard, the new president, had himself been Winona's superintendent of schools for some time, and was a distinguished educator in his own right, he could make the situation work. The triumvirate continued to have an outstanding relationship.

Shepard shared a number of qualities of his predecessors. Like Ogden, he was a decorated Civil War veteran, having fought bravely and suffered wounds at the Battle of the Wilderness. (He regaled Winona students with his war stories well into the twentieth century.) Like Phelps and Morey, he believed in educational reform and kept current with the latest theories of pedagogy. A stern disciplinarian (he would enter a classroom and, if he disliked the quality of the lesson being taught, would seize the chalk from the instructor and finish the class himself), he instituted a tradition of weekly faculty meetings to help govern the college. He also was the first of Winona Normal's administrators to carry the title of president.

President Shepard and some of the faculty were particularly enamored of the ideas of two early to mid-nineteenth-century educational theorists, Friedrich Froebel and Johann Friedrich Herbart. Froebel's focus on the importance of early childhood development led to America's great educational experiment of the 1880s, in which Winona Normal School would play an important part.

For Froebel, the goal of education was to produce a citizen of good character with a firm moral foundation based on Christian values. The process of education cultivated the good citizen by providing positive experiences and social interactions. Behavior, in other words, could be molded in socially acceptable ways that would contribute to the betterment of society at large. To accomplish this objective, the education of a child had to begin at a very early age, when the child was most impressionable. Froebel also stressed the importance of forming positive images in a child's mind. (In the early nineteenth century, when he and Herbart published their works, the emphasis was on comprehending the rational mind, not the subconscious that Sigmund Freud would later declare to be so important.) Froebel's work on the minds of young children suggested that meaningful learning might occur at an age earlier than previously suspected. Was it possible that children four and five years of age were possessed of reason and could learn?

Froebel chose the word *kindergarten* (garden of children) for his early childhood program, because he believed in the importance of play in childhood development. Personally neglected as a child, Froebel had struggled through his early youth, knocking about for several years and even spending a while in debtor's prison because he owed money as a college student. Finally, in his early twenties he found his vocation when he was asked to teach at an experimental school. After a couple of years teaching, he determined to learn more at the feet of the master, Johann Pestalozzi, and he traveled to Switzerland to meet and work with him. Within a few years Froebel penned his most important work,

The Education of Man, and began teaching in a normal school. Ultimately, he abandoned this career in 1837 to found the first kindergarten, to put his ideas into action and perhaps to spare other children the sense of neglect he had felt in his youth.

Shepard and the Winona faculty were well acquainted with Froebel's ideas and needed only a suggestion to turn the theoretical into something practical. In recent years, other normal schools had begun to experiment with the idea of kindergarten, and President Shepard determined to bring the innovation to Winona as part of the model school. As a result, Winona established the first kindergarten west of the Mississippi, and Winona Normal soon created the first program for kindergarten teacher training in the state. Obviously, the introduction to kindergarten education was an important innovation for the state of Minnesota and a great benefit for the community. As with the model school, children had to pay tuition, so the kindergarten was also economically self-sufficient.

The normal school's kindergarten put into action Froebel's idea of the importance of play for childhood development. Of course, this play was not random; rather it was structured with an educational objective. Music, singing, and drawing (Winona had a faculty member teaching music as early as 1864 and art courses shortly thereafter) provided essential elements of the kindergarten curriculum because Froebel's ultimate aim was to guide the child's heart and head and to serve a moral purpose. Winona's kindergarten based on Froebel's model thus became an integral part of the normal school curriculum. Although Winona's kindergarten training program would undergo permutations and ultimately be eliminated as a stand-alone degree, from this point forward prospective elementary teachers had to learn how to instruct the youngest of children at the kindergarten age.

Today, of course, the importance of giving children a "head start" in education has become a standard idea. As Froebel (and Shepard) suggested, early education initiates the process of socialization, so important in an increasingly complex world. The kindergarten movement took root in the United States thanks in great part to pioneers like the president and faculty at Winona.

Although the new kindergarten marked the most innovative aspect of Winona Normal's development in the 1880s and 1890s, the more traditional normal school curriculum, which of course involved the vast majority of the students, continued to modernize as well. Although many of Pestalozzi's principles remained current, others were modified as part of the work of the second German philosopher and educational theorist, Johan Friedrich Herbart, revered by Shepard and his faculty. Known as the founder of modern scientific pedagogy, Herbart, who had spent time with Pestalozzi and endorsed much of his theory, came to believe that the interaction of ideas and education could be reduced to a mathematical formula and that young students could be trained through a system ultimately known as Herbartianism. This system relied on five basic ideas. First came *preparation*, where students were prepared to understand new concepts by relating them to previously mastered material. Second was *presentation*, where the instructor used concrete examples to teach the new concept. Third, the teacher used *association* to relate the new subject area to other ideas that the student already knew. In the fourth stage adolescents learned to make *generalizations* from the examples studied. Finally, with *application*, students had to put the concepts into use. By the use of the term *application*, Herbart did not want to suggest that all education was utilitarian or vocational; rather, he meant that the new ideas could well be an applied life lesson.

For Herbart and his proponents, who dominated the field of education in the United States at the end of the nineteenth century, the principles of pedagogy were scientific, incorporating the new ideas of psychology and leading to the inclusion of courses in developmental psychology in the curriculum. Later critics like John Dewey would find Herbart's ideas too mechanistic, and early in the twentieth century they fell into disrepute. President Shepard, however, like most educators of his age, was enamored of Herbartianism as was his faculty. Hence Winona's curriculum took on this pragmatic bent, fitting in well with the need for elementary school teachers to prepare their students for a life of work in the factory or the home. (Classes in home economics became part of the curriculum in the 1890s.)

But Shepard could not spend all of his time in the ozone layer of educational theory; both he and the next president, Dr. Jesse Millspaugh, had to deal with practical issues as well. Shepard convinced policymakers in the state legislature that the normal school diploma ought to deliver more clout, and in the 1890s the degree was made the equivalent of the teaching license. By 1918 students were banned from attending Winona Normal to receive a high school diploma alone; they had to commit to additional training with the intention to pursue the normal school degree. Even as standards for admission and graduation toughened over time, enrollments increased to over three hundred students. The faculty grew in number as well to twenty-three, and began organizing into departments during Shepard's presidency. Building projects were undertaken, including two wings added to Old Main in 1894 that allowed an expansion of the model school, an increase in the number of classrooms and laboratories, and the addition of a gymnasium, supervised quite logically by the English Department. (A retired English professor reports with glee that his department continued to demonstrate its mastery at sports over the Athletic Department at least through the 1980s.) The English Department further demonstrated its versatility when one of its members, Charlotte Chorpenning, wrote the words to the alma mater sung at every graduation.

Concurrent with the exuberance and self-confidence of the Gilded Age and the new US imperialist expansionism was also the introspection that marked the final decade of the century. The city of Winona prospered, as evidenced by the great Victorian mansions that still encircle Windom Park and run up and down Broadway and Wabasha Streets, their owners often lumber barons, mill owners, bankers, or land speculators. As Minnesota matured along with other parts of the upper Midwest, the noted American historian Frederick Jackson Turner declared the closing of the frontier as a phenomenon in American history. With that closing, the state began to develop new industries, particularly in the growing metropolis of Minneapolis. Winona, too, enjoyed its share of entrepreneurs like the Watkins family, who sent door-to-door salesmen throughout the United States, peddling spices and liniment that had been prepared in a Winona factory. The coming of industry to Minnesota in turn created a demand for a new type of teacher, an educator who could prepare both elementary and high school students for careers in industry (before 1912 normal school graduates could teach at any level if a School Board would hire them. After that date, the state drew a distinction between the training required for the two professions). As usual, the normal school met the challenge by adding to the curriculum a new course of study in industrial arts.

Carving out courses in the industrial arts area was an outgrowth of Morey's work in building laboratory sciences, which had always contained a practical component. Students at the "common schools," as the elementary schools were called in the nineteenth century, needed a practical frame of mind if they were to be successful in working in the new factories. Girls as well as boys needed more practical skills, and so teachers also needed to know something about sewing and cooking. Penmanship and basket weaving formed essential parts of the curriculum, hard as that is for the modern educator to grasp. Well-known faculty member Theda Gildemeister, who labored at Winona Normal for over thirty years, developed these new courses for women beginning in 1898. One of the strengths of the school, then, was its growing ability to prepare teachers to meet the greater society's needs as that society changed and became more complex.

Along with the Gilded Age's emphasis on industrial growth and productivity, or perhaps as an offshoot of that development, American entrepreneurs began to look overseas for markets and raw materials. By the end of the nineteenth century the United States embarked on its quest for empire, and the results of the Spanish-American War would transfer control of Cuba, Puerto Rico, and the Philippines from that former great power to the rising one. On a relative scale, Winona Normal participated in the nation's growing sense of a larger world community, particularly with its interaction with Argentina in the 1870s, 1880s, and 1890s. One of that country's greatest presidents, Domingo F. Sarmiento, had, during a time of inevitable exile, befriended the United States' best-known leader of the normal school movement, Horace Mann of Massachusetts. Much taken with the notion of the normal school, Sarmiento had, on becoming president of Argentina, dedicated great efforts to creating a universal free public school system in that country and normal schools in every province, staffed with graduates from normal schools. Issuing calls to the entire world, Argentina sought sixty-one normal school graduates to lead its elementary schools and normal schools. Winona responded with numbers larger than any other American institution. Fifteen graduates of Winona Normal as well as William Stearns, the first faculty member, spent many years enriching the world of children and staffing normal schools in this rapidly developing South American country, whose geography and history resembled that of the United States. Even today, Argentine school children remember their names—for a number of schools are named for Winona graduates—and celebrate their contributions.

Simultaneously, however, one of the most interesting developments at Winona Normal was occurring off campus. Ever since the time that Clara Caswell's buckboard had carried her over the rough Burns Valley Road into Winona, the normal school had wrestled with the challenge of housing its students. As long as enrollments remained low, individuals could board with families or relatives and be certain of warm, secure surroundings and healthful meals. But as the popularity of Winona Normal increased and more and more students gained admission to the college, a pressing demand arose for housing. Once again the local community provided the answer. More specifically, the daughter of one of the local entrepreneurs, Miss M. F. Inglis, first rented and then bought a building near Old Main and opened a private boarding house for the purpose of housing female students. This new private dormitory, called the Normal Home, had a purpose beyond that of merely providing students a place to live. As one president stated somewhat later, the purpose of the dormitory was to socialize women whose "home life has been faulty and crude, and where social habits tend to be unladylike and coarse." Miss Inglis's dormitory schooled the girls in the social graces, and the Normal Home served the college well for almost thirty years, providing a residence for students at a very modest rate. In addition, Miss Inglis generously donated her profits to the Student Loan Fund, which began in 1894 as a loan program to help second- and third-year students who found themselves short of cash to complete their education. No state monies entered this fund, which came exclusively from Miss Inglis's gifts and graduating class gifts, a tradition firmly entrenched by the 1890s. As a result of Miss Inglis's work, Winona Normal began moving in the direction of becoming a residential campus.

By the end of the nineteenth century, Winona Normal had achieved a degree of prestige and was certainly current and innovative. Responding to the demands of the Gilded Age and the Age of Imperialism, the school took on a more practical bent as the teaching curriculum incorporated pragmatic subjects beyond the traditional three Rs and science. Keeping pace with the latest educational theories of Herbartianism and the kindergarten movement, President Shepard and the faculty, many of whom in the model school continued to be graduates of the prestigious Oswego program, advanced the school significantly. Nothing less could have been expected from Shepard. He achieved even greater fame in educational circles after retiring from the presidency in 1898 because of his increasing deafness. Elected as the permanent secretary of the National Education Association (still America's most prestigious education association), Shepard built an addition to his home where the NEA maintained its headquarters until he resigned in 1912.

When Dr. Shepard resigned his presidency, Winona Normal had the good fortune to select as its fifth president Dr. Jesse Millspaugh who had earned his medical degree at the University of Pennsylvania. Like Ogden, however, his physical infirmities had caused him to give up his first profession and turn to teaching. He made quite a reputation for himself as the superintendent of schools in Salt Lake City, bringing with him the idea of graded schools, kindergarten, and a host of teachers trained in Eastern normal schools. When offered the presidency of Winona Normal School in 1898, Millspaugh leapt at the opportunity for he had innovative ideas as well. Believing that adults should be physically as well as mentally fit (after all, this was the era of Theodore Roosevelt), he introduced courses in physical education to the curriculum. Other ambitious dreams—new buildings, new dormitories—flashed through his mind, but he resigned in 1904 to become the first president at what today is UCLA.

The end of the nineteenth century had been a time of growth and evolution for the institution. At critical junctures, the community of Winona reaffirmed its tradition of support for the normal school, helping the physical plant to grow and providing the first informal dormitory.

No longer threatened with fiscal disaster, Winona Normal was a truly distinctive institution that had made its mark. Often the first normal school in the state to react to the newest ideas of educational philosophy, Winona made sure its faculty remained well trained and dedicated to the mission of the school, even as that mission shifted slightly in these decades. For example, Winona State originated the idea of summer school in 1897 ("The Winona Plan" for continuous sessions as it was called then) until jealous rivals encouraged the State Normal School Board to shut down the enterprise because the other normal schools could not afford the sessions. To facilitate the plan, Winona Normal shifted from semesters to quarters and the others followed suit eventually. As admission standards tightened, the faculty sought to increase the rigor and length of the program and to lessen the dual role of Winona Normal as both a teacher-training institute and a high school. In a sense, Winona's presidents in this era were among the very best in its history; certainly they were nationally known figures, which was not the case with most of their successors. For better or worse (unfortunately all too often the latter) the time had come for a different type of leadership, one that would make Winona just one campus in a larger system, but which would still permit interesting local traditions to evolve starting in the early twentieth century.

The Struggle with Mediocrity: Winona State from 1904 to 1964

Chapter 2

The excesses of the Gilded Age and the ruthless conquests of the Age of Imperialism caused a twentieth-century reaction in American politics known as the Progressive Movement which helped pave the way for the New Deal in the 1930s. Leaders concerned with the inequities faced by farmers and laborers in the factories proposed reforms like the forty-hour workweek, compensation programs for injured workers, safety requirements for factories, the graduated income tax, and regulations that would purify the food supply. The Great Lakes states, including Minnesota, were in the vanguard of the Progressive Movement. Change was in the air in St. Paul, where farmers marched on the capitol demanding fairer prices and labor leaders besieged politicians demanding greater benefits.

While these changes were transformative for American society, Winona Normal did not keep pace for a variety of reasons. Even as John Dewey proposed great reforms in educational theory, talking about pragmatic forms of education and the relationship between education and the values of democracy, Winona Normal's latest president was not in the vanguard of educational theory. A member of the faculty handpicked for the presidency by Charles Morey, who still served on the State Normal School Board, football coach and Phelps Model School head Guy Maxwell seems to have had little interest in intellectual matters. He was, however, a figure of great stability and strong moral character, serving as president for thirty-five years and setting in motion much of the construction of the institution's physical plant. Beneath his gruff exterior, Maxwell was a kindly man. After his death, for example, his son found evidence suggesting that Dr. Maxwell had helped to pay the tuition of a number of needy students.

For better or worse two presidents, Guy Maxwell (1904–38) and Nels Minné (1944–67) dominated Winona State's history over the ensuing six decades. In this same period, Winona State became thoroughly enmeshed within a system that sought to centralize authority in the State Normal School Board and its successors. The results of these two changes were mixed. On the positive side, institutionalization meant that Winona State acquired stability; the idea of a college in Winona became a fixture in the minds of most Minnesotans. On the negative side, Winona State experienced the leveling effect of that relationship, and much of the academic curriculum became quite standardized even as the school evolved into a four-year college. Change occurred slowly as Winona Normal walled itself from the world of progress and innovation and instead merely reacted to external forces. As such, the school lost its ability at times to meet society's changing needs. Yet Winona State would manage nevertheless to overcome catastrophes of biblical proportions. Wars, fires, famine, depression—all laid siege to Winona Normal, which withstood these buffets and tempests perhaps because of its institutionalized status. The period of growing institutionalization and uninspiring leadership might be characterized in terms of the Clint Eastwood movie, *The Good, the Bad, and the Ugly*. Because change occurred so gradually during these decades, this chapter has been arranged topically in those terms rather than chronologically.

In its early years, Winona Normal had achieved success in all five areas that have been the constant themes of its history: its innovative role in higher education; its forward-looking leadership endorsing educational experimentation; its successful partnership with the city in constructing a physical plant and a positive social environment; its fulfillment of the social contract to provide teachers for the state; and its evolving academic standards. During the next sixty years, the school managed to advance only two of these five objectives, maintaining its partnership with the city and continuing to fulfill its social contract by graduating teachers and other good citizens (the "good"). The institution's failure in the other three represents the "bad." Without disparaging our graduates from that era, a success rate of 40 percent suggests that Winona State stagnated to a significant degree. What the college did accomplish in these years was good management if not good leadership. This chapter will first look at the students and the college's traditions and extracurricular activities, which helped Winona State's graduates become good teachers and citizens, and to fulfill their social contract with the state. The "good" will conclude with an examination of the growing physical plant, the ongoing positive relationships between the town and the campus, the management successes of Presidents Maxwell and Minné, the changing curriculum, and the enrollment growth of the 1950s and 1960s.

The Good: The Social Contract

Traditions

Winona State continued to fulfill its social contract, providing well-qualified elementary schoolteachers, and as a result, prospered during the Roaring Twenties. Enrollments reached record levels, especially as the state authorized normal schools to offer four-year degrees, which over time increased in popularity. (For years Winona enjoyed the largest graduating class in the system, although St. Cloud began to eclipse Winona in the 1930s, and by 1946 Winona would be the smallest of the six state teachers' colleges.) But the new State Teachers' College Board—all the state normal schools became teachers' colleges in 1921—exacted a heavy price for the promotion in status; because of the new "systems approach," individual distinctions between campuses diminished. Nevertheless, the college settled into stability during these decades, the academic year took on a discernible rhythm as Winona State developed a series of meaningful traditions that would provide it with some individual identity. Some traditions clearly began as normal administrative events (the Fall Welcome, Commencement); others appear to have been faculty initiatives; and still others seem to have been created through joint student, faculty, and alumni efforts. Over the years, these traditions gained in importance and, because they boosted school spirit, helped further the educational mission of the college.

To overcome the anxieties of new students away from home for the first time, the normal school experimented with an orientation program called "Big Sister–Little Sister" (so called because 90 percent of the enrollment was female) wherein each senior (second-year student) took a junior (first-year student) under her wing and introduced her to a circle of friends. Near the end of September, the president presided at the annual Faculty Reception, billed as one of the two fanciest and most formal events on campus, and akin to today's Convocation ceremony. New students passed through the formal reception line, where they met the president, his wife, the long-serving dean of women, Florence Richards (1912–1943), and many, if not all, of the faculty. The college served suitable refreshments, and then everyone was invited to attend the dance, which Miss Richards chaperoned. (Today the sexual harassment officer might frown at this student-faculty mixer, but these were more innocent or naive times.) Winona billed itself as a very friendly campus, an echo of today's theme of "your home away from home," and the Faculty Reception was designed to make new students feel that they were part of the college community. In 1926, the faculty initiated a formal advising system that involved all faculty except the president and the two deans of men and women. A formal orientation course followed for the month of September, which included topics like study skills, college history, society and the environment, and "use and abuse of the library," as well as an introduction to the community.

Late in the 1920s, a modest form of hazing during orientation began. Early on these initiation rites caused no bodily harm and were designed to instill school spirit. First-year men wore green (sometimes purple) beanies for the first term (green, of course, symbolizing inexperience) and carried books, opened doors, and completed chores for upperclassmen. Women, still between two-thirds and three-fourths of all enrollees, experienced much milder treatment. One year the upperclasswomen required the new girls to wear their make-up on one side of their face only and different colored shoes, which must have been a bit embarrassing. Another year the frosh had to push peanuts across a floor with their noses. By and large Winona escaped the dangerous hazing rituals that eventually became nationwide scandals in the 1950s and 1960s, although men protested the paddlings that crept into the rituals in the late 1930s. Most pranks were simply good-natured fun. Officially, hazing ended with the beginning of winter quarter, when the "freshmen" were redesignated as "first-year students."

Another ritual marked the end of formal orientation in September. Friendship Day, the brainchild of kindergarten director Louise Sutherland and the students in the YWCA Club, took place during one of the daily chapel periods, and began with a musical piece or two and a short poetry reading. Then Miss Sutherland gave her annual talk (this occurred for more than twenty years) on the meaning and importance of friendship. The texts of her speeches have not survived, but her audience remembered these talks fondly for years. She encouraged the lonely to reach out and asked all students to respect their peers. Then the gathered group sang the alma mater. As the students filed out of the assembly, each of the first-year women (sometimes both the women and men) received a freshly picked wildflower, usually an aster from the fields around Garvin Heights, as a symbol of friendship from her upper-class sister. Friendship Day played an important part in the college's objective of making newcomers feel welcome. In short, providing another moment that united the student and faculty communities (at that point there were between 350 and 500 students), it became an important ritual.

Beginning in 1922, Winona celebrated a third autumn tradition, an annual Homecoming. (A first Homecoming had occurred in 1919 to mark the return of soldiers from World War I.) Instead of scheduling the event early, as the university currently does to take advantage of brisk yet sunny weather, in this era Winona followed the national trend and scheduled Homecoming for mid-November. This soon became the major celebratory occasion for the fall. Homecoming Weekend began with a "snake dance," so-called because the participants snaked their way through downtown, followed by a bonfire where the pep squad led students, faculty, and alumni through the school cheers and the College Rouser or fight song. Sometimes the Wenonah Players performed their fall play this weekend.

As it does today, the Homecoming Parade occurred on Saturday morning, followed by the big football game against a major rival such as Mankato or St. Cloud. In the Guy Maxwell years (1904–1939), Winona generally fared well in football since it managed to enroll more men than most of the other teachers' colleges and because it occasionally recruited an outstanding athlete like Tom "Moon" Mullins. In addition to starring at football, Mullins won popular approval because of his modesty. In 1929, for example, he withdrew his nomination for "Most Representative Man" because he believed he had missed too many chapel services. After graduation, he became a very active member of the Alumni Association for many years. As rivalries grew, Winona students pulled stunts like kidnapping the St. Cloud mascot (a goat) and keeping it until St. Cloud beat Winona in the annual contest. (This took three years.) After the game, students attended the Homecoming Dance, which beginning in the late 1930s, crowned one young woman as the Homecoming Queen. World War II temporarily de-emphasized the importance of the queen and the dance because of the absence of men on campus—and moved the whole event to February—but thereafter the dance regained prominence until the late 1970s.

Lesser fall holidays included Halloween, Thanksgiving, and Christmas. Halloween provided the occasion for a party and dance, and of course, costumes appropriate for the occasion. Although most students left Winona to spend Thanksgiving at home, a few remained in the dormitories, where they cooked a traditional meal and enjoyed each other's company. Of course, not all the faculty left the city to spend Thanksgiving elsewhere, so these dormitory feasts provided another opportunity for student-faculty interaction. Before the break, the college held a Christmas party for all students and faculty, replete with festive food. In addition, many of the young women continued the tradition of providing for the wants of others, by making or purchasing small gifts that could be shared with the less fortunate children of the community.

The college always enjoyed some form of celebration in February, although its nature changed over the decades. Initially, the students and faculty participated in the city's Winter Carnival, then, for some twenty to thirty years, students decided to run their own festival. The brainchild of the pep club Die-No-Mo, founded to create fundraising events for athletic clubs, homecoming expenses, and high school recruiting, the Winter Carnival brightened up what some would argue are the dreariest days of the year in Minnesota. Sponsoring games, a talent show, a skit, and a dance, the annual event provided some excitement for the beginning of the second portion of the school year. In the age of vaudeville, Die-No-Mo's members performed juggling feats, sang, and danced, and of course, satirized the faculty in droll skits. However, this tradition appears to have died out in the 1940s, with the club's demise occurring shortly thereafter.

Because Winona winters were no balmier then they had been in the nineteenth century, Winter Carnival in whatever form provided a welcome diversion from the cold. Die-No-Mo's carnival was eventually replaced by a junior class event. Much of the hoopla focused on the selection of Miss Snowflake and her court (portrayed in 1947 wearing bathing suits while on skis or a toboggan), and the Winter Carnival Dance. The revived Winter Carnival also featured lots of outdoor activities—toboggan races, snow volleyball, snow sculptures, and broom hockey. In these years the city of Winona graciously allowed the students to use Lake Park for their events.

Later in the spring came the Annual Prom. Beginning in 1927, the prom involved many students in its organization. The Art Club designed the decorations and organized the event. The 1927 prom focused on the various nationalities represented on campus—twenty-two different European ethnicities. Drawing several hundred students (out of fewer than five hundred), the prom clearly proved a very popular student activity. Themes for later proms included the Arctic, Jungle Tales, China, and Disney Characters (Mickey Mouse and Donald Duck had just hit the screens in the mid-1930s). Even in the middle of World War II, with almost no men on campus, the prom tradition continued, with the women dressing as "the most romantic couples in history." After the war, the Spring Prom drew upwards of five hundred students and a few faculty. As long-established tradition demanded, then President Nels Minné and his wife headed the formal reception line. During the 1950s, extended hours allowed students to stay out until 12:30 a.m., and the prom's location at the Oaks, the popular Minnesota City restaurant and club renown throughout the Midwest (the Three Stooges once dined there), made for even later curfews.

Prom eventually became part of the larger May Fete, or May Field Day. At this time of year, the students elected "Alma Mater," the graduating senior woman who "best represented the college physically, mentally, and morally." She became the central figure in a stylized Festival of Light pageant, which glorified education. Other performers sang or danced, and the assembly ended with all students and faculty singing the alma mater. Not to be outdone, the men demanded equal time, so a similar election took place for the campus's "Most Representative Man." By the late 1920s both appeared in the Festival of Light, with "Alma Mater," now renamed "Most Representative Woman," receiving a crown as her part of the ceremony ended. After this exceedingly formal ceremony lost favor, the selection of the most representative man and woman became an integral part of the annual prom activities. (Today, Winona State University continues to celebrate this tradition with its election of "Mr. WSU" and "Ms. WSU" in the spring). After being crowned, the "representative couple" paraded around the dance floor, followed by the class presidents and their dates. In sum, the Annual Prom became the highlight of the college students' spring social season—in part because it was the only officially sponsored student activity allowed to conclude at the unseemly late hour of 11:00 p.m. in the 1920s.

Commencement week concluded the regular academic year. Initially a seven-day celebration of the students' transition from academia to the world of work, Senior Week began with a college-sponsored dinner to which alumni were invited on the Sunday before graduation, followed by a formal sermon at chapel. On Wednesday, seniors heard a concert, while Thursday, Class Night, saw seniors entertain others with a class play ranging from the classical (*The Tempest* in 1923) to the informal skit that marked the end of the year in 1936. For the entire week seniors wore their formal academic regalia. On Class Night the president of the senior class handed the "Loving Cup" to the president of the junior class, and the seniors presented their class gift to the college. Meanwhile, the faculty and administrators organized the Friday Commencement ceremony. Beginning in 1933, the highest honors, the Purple Key, went to the ten or fewer students who had the highest grade point averages in the college and who were involved in four or more extracurricular activities. Purple Key remained the most competitive honor, and its recipients wore a special pin at graduation.

Other traditions occurred during the summer. During these decades, summer school enrollments nearly equaled the enrollments of the regular academic year, probably because of increasingly tough licensure requirements for teachers. Hundreds of local teachers flocked to take summer courses at Winona State Teachers' College; faculty were expected to teach unless they had some alternate plan of activity. Summer enrollments remained high for decades, proving the wisdom of the "continuous enrollment" quarter-based system that President Irwin Shepard proposed in the 1890s. Naturally, students also created and participated in campus life during the summer. Speakers came to campus to enlighten students about world culture or world events. Once the campus held a Chautauqua event featuring William Jennings Bryan's daughter; another time an astronomer held forth. The students probably preferred the picnic, which usually took place at Garvin Heights Park, and the annual Mississippi River cruise, after that event was shifted from Fall Orientation. Hundreds of people jammed the boat (Winona citizens and alums must have been invited also), and sometimes tardy students had to leap aboard as the paddlewheel pulled out. Once on deck, students could play games like shuffleboard and quoits, listen to a faculty member talk about the river, squeeze onto the crowded dance floor, or just eat a picnic lunch.

Extracurricular Activities

Some college traditions evolved serendipitously, like world-class musical events and a speaker series. The speaker series dated back to the founding of the college, when people like Horace Greeley ("Go west, young man") delivered addresses in the old normal school building. Later orators included Henry Ward Beecher, Wendell Philips, the muck-raking illustrator Thomas Nast, and Jeanette Rankin, a former US representative from Montana who voted against the nation's entry into World War I and World War II. A temperance movement talk drew a big crowd as many questioned the wisdom of trying to outlaw the consumption of alcoholic beverages. A reformed criminal described the problems of cities caused by "pool halls, gun houses, and tough dance halls," where the "scum of the city congregate."

The campus hosted annually one or two major performers like Ricardo Martin (billed as America's greatest tenor), the Minneapolis Symphony, the Chicago Opera Company, and Swiss bell ringers. (There is no mention of jazz or other contemporary music forms.) During the Depression the internationally known violinist Toscha Seidel performed in Winona, allegedly because tough economic times reduced the fee he normally charged. By 1936, however, the college regularized these cultural experiences under the auspices of the Community Concert Series. A portion of the student's activity fee supported the series. In addition, the college sold tickets to the community at $5 per season, which when added to the student fees, raised a total of about $900, enough to field four quality concerts annually. As a result of the joint effort, the college brought singers to the campus like Helen Jepson (the star of the Metropolitan Opera Company), Paul Robeson, and the Von Trapp Family (whose story is told in *The Sound of Music*). At the same time, Winona recruited its own excellent student performers. The 1930s were the decade of students Everett and Hal Edstrom (who later founded the Hal Leonard Corporation, the world's largest music publishing company) and what would become the Hal Leonard Band. With the enthusiastic support of President Guy Maxwell, who wanted a college band to stir the crowds at athletic events, the Edstrom brothers purchased instruments, recruited performers, and played in all sorts of venues around the Midwest, bringing renown to Winona State's pep band and Music Department.

Athletics also built school spirit and a sense of community, and President Maxwell, a former coach, believed in the value of sports themselves. In addition, he saw the development of intercollegiate sports as a way to attract men to the campus and the teaching profession. Not that the women were not vigorously involved in athletics such as basketball, swimming, dance, baseball, tennis, hiking, and volleyball. (The school physician particularly recommended the latter form of exercise because "it raises the head, puts the shoulders back, and expands the chest.") As occurred so typically in these times, men's sports quickly crowded the women off the docket. Even though the Student Athletic Association granted an equal number of seats to both men and women with the chair rotating between the genders annually, the men received two-thirds of the budget. After all, the reasoning went, the men played the more expensive intercollegiate sports that required travel and fancier uniforms. (The original purple-and-white uniforms with *N* on them for *Normal* were eventually replaced with uniforms with a *W*.) Over the years the men's athletic teams had the usual ups and downs. Although one year the basketball team went undefeated and took down Mankato by lopsided 35 to 6 and 36 to 5 scores, a few years later the football team took its lumps, losing to La Crosse 101 to 0 in its first game and not faring as well as that in the rematch! (The coach was not fired; in fact, he remained a very well-respected faculty member.) What characterized Winona athletics in these early years was not a winning tradition necessarily, but a very high participation rate.

Of course, having intercollegiate sports teams mandated the need for a nickname for the college, although this changed over time. In the late 1920s somebody hung the moniker "The Peds" (presumably short for pedagogists, or teachers) on the athletic teams, a nickname that persisted in common usage through the early war years and even into the 1950s. As early as the 1930s students sought a more colorful name such as rival colleges had adopted—also downstream rival LaCrosse State Teachers' College had already become The Peds. For a while the teams were called "The Purple." In 1936 the college held a contest to select a nickname. Student voters could choose from the Purple Panthers, the Warriors, the Windians, the Eagles, the Werewolves, and the Purple Eagles. Ultimately, a plurality chose the Warriors, with Werewolves running a close second. Nevertheless, the nickname Warriors did not really become universally accepted until the 1950s as "Peds" very slowly faded out.

As the years passed, sports continued to contribute to the lives of many Winona State students. The football team enjoyed a couple of championship years in the early 1960s, and a few athletes entered the draft for the rapidly expanding National Football League, including Jerry Weidemeier, who played tackle and also won the National Small College Wrestling Championship three times. Baseball became the king of all sports at Winona State. During the 1950s, the men's team won the league championship for six consecutive seasons under the leadership of Coach Luther McCown. By the early 1960s the team ran off another string of championships, led by young men who would make their careers in various areas at Winona State, people like Gary Grob, Charlie Zane, Jon Kosidowski, and Bob Lietzau. President Maxwell and many others asserted that athletics helped to build character and good sportsmanship. Hence, an editorial eloquently condemned rowdy students who made noise while a WSU opponent attempted a free throw. (How far the values of good sportsmanship have diminished over the decades!)

Other clubs played important roles in student lives. The Radio Club allowed students broadcast opportunities with a local station, KWNO, one afternoon a week. Beginning a longstanding tradition, the Art Club traveled to Chicago to see museums and plays and attend the ballet. The International Students Club, founded in 1962, emerged. By then, "foreign" students were not limited to Asian-American Hawaiians as was the case in the 1930s, but included Iranians, Filipinos, Germans, Lebanese, and of course, Norwegians. Beginning shortly after the turn of the century, the drama club, the Wenonah Players, put on many plays including one by Charlotte Chorpenning, all well-attended, even though tickets cost the outlandish price of a dime apiece. Of course ticket prices and the texts of the plays changed considerably over the decades.

Music traditions changed. Although Fred Heyer, a popular music professor who had performed with the Hal Leonard Band, and his swing band remained popular in the early 1950s, classical concerts lost favor. Because of poor attendance, these concerts caused students to question whether their activity money ought to be spent on the community concert series. After 1962, student government sponsored the occasional pop concert. For example, in the fall of 1963 the Four Freshmen drew a crowd of twenty-one hundred people as they performed some of their hit songs. A new talent discovered on the *Arthur Godfrey Show* (the precursor of *American Idol*) also drew applause. Likewise, the number of speakers coming to campus declined. Humorous and famous speakers still drew respectable crowds. Paul Harvey (news commentator), Carey McWilliams (early anthropologist of the Southwest), and John Braine (author of *Room at the Top*, a novel converted into an Oscar-winning film) all attracted student interest, as did Maria Von Trapp (the stepmother of the Von Trapp Family Singers). Top scientists like Wernher Von Braun and Linus Pauling also visited Winona State.

Student government also became part of the college's traditions. Limited student participation in governance in an advisory capacity began in the latter Maxwell years. Apparently, the president and the two deans ruled the college with an iron fist (if in a velvet glove) until 1927, when students requested a "Representative Council." Initially consisting of the two deans, three faculty at large, the presidents and vice presidents of the upper classes, and the freshman class president, the group's charge was "to promote the scholastic and moral tone of the school." (The makeup of the body would change as the college transitioned to a four-year institution.) Soon, however, the Representative Council strayed from these strict guidelines and discussed controversial issues such as the abolition of daily chapel, a very popular student demand. (Some five or six faculty had refused to participate in chapel as well.) President Maxwell was persuaded to reduce assemblies to three times a week (students being responsible for the content of one of these presentations) after the Council produced evidence that this was a national trend. The group also appointed university committees, supervised committee work, approved new clubs, wrote and amended the student handbook, and recruited prospective students once a year. Members of the Representative Council also demanded that student parties and dances last later, saying the sounds of "Home, Sweet Home" rang out much too soon (curfew was 10:30 except for Prom Night), and this in turn encouraged students to patronize local bars that stayed open until midnight or 12:30. Students also agitated for a more liberal policy on "cuts," the number of absences they could sustain before failing a course, and requested a study day between the end of classes and the beginning of final examinations. In short, during the 1930s and 1940s students felt free to render advice to the college administration, but the administration remained very authoritarian. This would be true through the mid-1960s although during World War II students demanded and received more representation on the Council. As their role increased and that of the faculty and deans decreased, the Representative Council evolved to the current Student Senate system.

The Physical Plant

During these sixty years, the college maintained its close relationship to the community, another important success. At least through the 1930s, the city of Winona participated quite actively in the funding of the physical plant, and students continued to serve the city and especially its children well. Construction activity began in 1909 just east of where Somsen Hall stands, where a structure called Ogden Hall was built for use as a kindergarten, gymnasium, and library. (This small structure stood until the 1950s.) Six years later, the state appropriated the money for Phelps Hall, a sign of the growing need for physical space. Next came the construction of Somsen Hall, discussed later in this chapter. In 1938 Maxwell also arranged for building the "new" library that bore his name—one of the few public buildings in Minnesota constructed during the 1930s. Because of circumstances discussed below, President Maxwell, knowing that the state could hardly help during the Depression, came up with the idea of a joint venture for the library project. He secured a Federal Public Works Administration grant for $41,000 that covered 45 percent of the costs and raised an additional $50,000 from twenty-eight Winona businessmen. Once again the community had stepped in to help the college. Interestingly, Maxwell Hall was located off campus initially, although the state moved quickly to acquire the property on which it stood. The new library building opened shortly after Guy Maxwell's death in 1939. Very quickly students asked that the college hire a second librarian so that the facility could remain open at night when most students wanted to study.

Community members may have felt loyalty to the institution in part because of the Phelps Model School, where some of their children were educated. The model school not only linked the campus to the city, but it remained one of the few innovative entities on campus. Unlike the days of Phelps and Shepard, the model school did not experiment with daring new philosophies, but its faculty did experiment pragmatically with the teaching/learning process; ideas like modular scheduling and making music visual that they shared with hundreds of teacher-education students observing them.

Maxwell also undertook the construction of the first dormitories, named Morey and Shepard Halls. (Student life in the dorms was regimented: mandatory study halls from 2:00 to 5:00 p.m. and 7:30 to 10:00 p.m. Monday through Saturday; only one light lit in a room, and no running up and down the stairs!) Even in the 1940s, the residence halls were filled to capacity. After World War II, enrollments more than doubled, forcing more and more students to live in the community. No longer could the city easily absorb the college crowd which caused tension. In addition to the library and dorms, Maxwell acquired more land for athletic fields, fittingly his real legacy. He dreamed of the day when the state would build Winona a field house and make the college a real sports power. Maxwell valued participatory athletics for everybody, and his ultimate vision was to make Winona State the finest preparer of physical education teachers in the state. Maxwell gloried in the triumphs of the intercollegiate sports teams and emphasized sports as a means of attracting male enrollment. Further campus expansion had to wait until the 1950s, however.

Managing the Campus

Good presidents successfully manage enrollments and budgets as a part of furthering the educational mission of the college. Managing budgets began as a simple task (the state funded one faculty position for every sixteen students), but after the 1930s things became more complex, with addition of tuition and fees. Still Maxwell and Minné did well. Beginning with the early years of the Depression, the state of Minnesota had authorized the teachers' colleges to charge tuition—a modest $16 per quarter at first, but incrementally increasing over time. In 1953, tuition and fees amounted to $104 per quarter, an increase that students protested on the grounds that 40 percent of the body of students were the children of mechanics and laborers, whose finances were stretched to meet the burden. Including room and board, only three years later the cost of a year at Winona State had increased to $1,300, consistent with national figures for like institutions. Students—and parents—bore an ever-larger share as state appropriations declined early in the 1950s. President Minné and students protested the frugality of the state legislature, but had to accept the inevitability of a large tuition increase. As the state once again began to take more seriously its duty to provide public higher education, appropriations improved in the 1960s.

Students' reaction to the cost of higher education remained consistent. According to a survey that President Minné commissioned in 1958, the average Winona State student worked many hours, and with loans and family contributions paid 76 percent of the cost of his or her education. Student editorials over the years bemoaned tuition increases, arguing that they limited access to higher education. Yet enrollments increased continuously. President Minné, who had prided himself on knowing every student by name in the 1940s, now found the task impossible. At times the students' resistance to higher costs and fees appeared shortsighted. For example, in 1961 the students opposed a $5 per quarter increase in the student activity fee intended to fund the construction of the student union. The following year the State College Board imposed the fee, although by then student opinion had mitigated somewhat because the planners had agreed to add state-of-the-art bowling alleys to the facility. Hence, Winona State's budget became a complex balancing act between state appropriation, tuition, and fees, making increasing enrollments ever more attractive as a means of assuring revenue.

Because parents after the 1930s shouldered a much greater financial burden for their child's education, President Minné decided that a special Parents' Day showcasing the campus might make them happier about their investment. In the fall of 1955, then, the college opened dorms to parents one weekend, fed them a meal, invited them to a football game, and provided music for a dance. These activities allowed parents to meet faculty and tour the campus, and Parents' Day has remained an important event to the present.

Despite budget issues, the college never forgot its mission to serve. As the student president of the class of 1920 said, "We have for the past two years been in the midst of those who were continually calling forth the best in us and giving the best of themselves. . . . With the guidance of our alma mater we have not only broadened our lives but deepened them to include charity for all." But as the teachers' college added new degrees and programs, it seemed to change its mission to serve the public good especially in the face of the mixed economy that emerged after World War II. In 1948, Winona State still marketed itself primarily as a teacher-preparation institution although its promotional materials stated that "the college exists not merely to supply professionally trained teachers, but also to provide those who attend here a broad, rich educational experience." By 1961, with the absence of any specific reference to teacher training, the new mission statement reflected Winona State's transition in the direction of a liberal arts and science college with select professional programs. "Winona State College is learning together in a community with a common goal." The mission had broadened significantly because of increased enrollment, rather than any planned restructuring of the institution. By the 1950s, not all Winona State students wanted to pursue careers in education, and the new mission reflected changing patterns of interest among students.

Enrollment increases had other effects. Even as the courses of study diversified, the education program grew. No longer could all teach under the watchful eye of the faculty at the Phelps Model School. As a result, the system of practice teaching in the Winona area public schools began in 1949, and eventually the model school would be forced to close.

Student services also had to change. No student service encountered more problems resulting from increasing enrollment than the Registrar's Office. No doubt the increased complexities of large enrollments contributed to Helen Pritchard's decision to retire in the 1950s after serving as registrar since 1916. By 1963, students nearly rioted over the college's preregistration policy, which had remained unchanged since Miss Pritchard's day. Students waited in a single line to receive an appointment time with their advisor, after which they returned to Somsen Hall and waited in another line to obtain their class cards to obtain their seats in classes. With two thousand students on campus, this procedure took a full day! After mulling over options like eliminating choices for first-year students and simply handing them a package of set courses, the administration finally decided to purchase newfangled IBM machines which printed class lists and eliminated one of the lines. (President Minné had opposed this technological advance, so WSU was the last of the state colleges to purchase such equipment.)

Not all of the new enrollment came on the Winona campus. Although Winona State had offered off-site classes, primarily in Rochester, since 1917, in the 1950s the college became more involved in extension coursework because of the need to provide additional training for in-service teachers, who now had to complete their four-year degree or forgo any advancement on the salary schedule. This legislation convinced the college to abandon its longstanding two-year rural education program, which in the 1920s and 1930s had supplied elementary teachers to "out-state" Minnesota. In any event, Winona State began offering courses in many communities in southeastern Minnesota as part of this outreach program. No doubt this program, coupled with Rochester's emergence as a large population center, led to the insidious idea that first found currency in the legislative session of 1958—to move the institution wholesale to Rochester. Although much of this discussion remained cloaked in secrecy, both President Minné and Resident Director (trustee) Sylvester J. Kryzsko, the president of the Winona National Bank, fought the idea. Supporters of transferring the campus to Rochester pointed to the generous gift of land offered by a local businessman, which would have solved the expansion problems faced by a landlocked campus. Instead, to counter this argument, Minné advocated for a land acquisition program in the next legislative session, which greatly increased the size of the Winona campus.

Expansion in the 1950s

Higher enrollments changed the face of the campus and led to the need to construct more facilities. Although President Guy Maxwell had overseen some additions to the physical plant during his long tenure, President Nels Minné presided over the greatest expansion in Winona State's history. As early as 1954, Minné forecast the need for many new buildings. He predicted that Winona State would enroll two thousand students by the late 1960s and later prophesized that enrollments would double between 1958 and 1970. (His estimates proved low in both instances.) Fortunately, policymakers agreed that investing in Minnesota's future by rapidly expanding higher education facilities made a great deal of sense, and did so through issuing bonds. Legislatures fully bonded instructional buildings, while residence halls, student activities buildings, and other income-producing buildings were eligible for revenue bonds, where the state provided only one-fourth of the money with the remainder raised by bonds to be repaid by revenues from room, board, or fees. By this method, the brainchild of Sylvester Kryzsko, the state, which faced similar expansion on all campuses, could construct significantly more buildings for its dollars. Awash with public money, the campus began its greatest period of physical growth.

A new indoor athletic facility, so essential to sound well-being in the cold Minnesota climate, began the construction boom. After being shuttled from Phelps Hall to Ogden to Somsen, athletics finally found a home in Memorial Hall and the two-thousand-seat McGown Gymnasium, named for longtime athletic director and baseball coach Luther McGown. To build this facility, President Minné persuaded the legislature to provide funds to demolish Ogden Hall, which had suffered damage in the great fire of 1922 (discussed later in this chapter), but had continued to be used for a number of purposes (library, classrooms, athletics, student activities, and bookstore, among others) over the ensuing thirty years. Shortly thereafter, in 1956, work began on Howell Hall, named for Etta Hudson Howell, a former education faculty member who bequeathed half of her estate to the college to provide scholarships for needy elementary education students. Originally intended to provide additional space for the Education Department in Phelps, Howell offered new classrooms, an entire floor of observation rooms, and a kitchen and lunchroom in the basement. No sooner had Howell Hall opened than construction began on the first of two additions to Maxwell Library, providing much needed space for the growing collection as well as study areas.

Classroom construction continued apace in the early 1960s. Once again, President Minné predicted the coming enrollment explosion and acted as advocate before the state legislature. During the 1959 session, he testified about the need for a science building, an arts building (including industrial arts), a heating plant, and a new facility for education. Within a very short time, Pasteur Hall rose from its foundations, billed as the finest science building in the state, at a cost of $1.25 million, including some new equipment. (This is the only building on campus named for someone with no connection to Winona State; the faculty committee was charged to select the name from among the great scientists of the world.) Minné did, however, insist on cheap construction. As originally equipped, neither Pasteur nor Watkins had telephones in faculty offices, only an intercom system. Office staff in Somsen ferried over telephone messages if they deemed them urgent. Nor, as noted later, was any great attention given to architectural aesthetics here or in any of the buildings constructed in this era. Finally, in 1964 two additional academic buildings opened. Gildemeister Hall, named for longtime education professor Theda Gildemeister, now housed the College of Education, freeing space in Phelps Hall for the new nursing program. Watkins Hall, named for the family of generous Winona benefactors who donated the art collection still to be seen in portions of Somsen and Minné Halls, became the home of the Art Department and the Industrial Education Department. Although enrollment growth would spur two additional academic buildings (the Performing Arts Center and Minné Hall) in the late 1960s and early 1970s, much of the current campus's architecture came into being under the leadership of President Minné.

As enrollments doubled, so did the need for student housing. Of course, not all students wanted to live in on campus, particularly the older, nontraditional students, some of whom were married veterans and accustomed to greater self-sufficiency. As a result, off-campus apartments surrounded the college, a phenomenon that continues well into the twenty-first century. But thanks to Resident Director Kryzsko's brainstorm, healthy revenues funded an explosion of new dorm construction; Old West, Prentiss, Lucas, and Richards Halls fell to the wrecking ball, to be replaced by modern dormitories (the Quad) bearing many of the same names. Additionally, two new housing units made their appearance: Conway Hall, named for Helen Conway, a WSU graduate and member of the State College Board, and Sheehan Hall, named for Resident Director Frank Sheehan, who had served two terms as trustee prior to Kryzsko. Never had the campus undergone such a physical transformation, and as former president Robert DuFresne entertainingly describes in his book, the sound of hammers, saws, and heavy equipment echoed across campus, while students tracked mud and dust from the projects everywhere. Other projects from revenue bond sources included Loughrey Field, named for WSU's oldest living letterman, Peter Loughrey of the class of 1900. (Interestingly Loughrey, a Spanish-American War veteran, had gone to the Philippines as a volunteer teacher in 1901, where he opened an elementary school for the newly freed former colony. He told WSU students in the 1960s about the difficulties of teaching Filipino students the three Rs, and also about the day he was required to bring them to witness a public hanging, so that they would learn about the US justice system.) Finally, revenue bonds paid for Kryzsko Common, completed in 1968.

The New Academic Programs

During the growth spurt of the 1950s, Winona State transformed itself from a teachers' college to a more general liberal arts and science institution. The name change of 1957, dropping *Teachers*, reflected a new emphasis on the liberal arts and sciences and the diminished importance of the education program. Many graduates now majored in purely academic disciplines and pursued a whole range of careers. The new majors—speech, history, English, business—still appeal to many of today's graduates. Psychology separated from the Department of Education as a discipline mature enough to merit its own major. The sciences, led by professors like Joe Emanuel and Cal Fremling in biology, and Fred Foss in chemistry, carved out distinctive academic disciplines. In 1964 the college introduced a nursing major, which appealed primarily to scientifically minded females. By then liberal arts and science graduates, like longtime Winona Mayor Jerry Miller, a history major, outnumbered the teachers' college graduates, another reason to discard the nickname "Peds."

The faculty transformed itself as well. Because of pressures from accrediting agencies, Winona State hired more PhDs as faculty. While old-timers like Willis Boots had served the English Department well for many years (and also taught biology), and Charles F. Jederman, a history professor, had laid the foundation for the modern department, the new faculty had generally more advanced graduate training. These professors, among them David Rislove (a Winona graduate who bridged the gap between athletics and academics), Jim and Ann Nichols (outstanding members of the English department and published authors), and Jim Eddy (lobbyist and environmental preservationist), would leave their mark on the college for the next two decades. Some faculty won great honors for their scholarship and professional activity. Dorothy Magnus, the grande dame of the Theater Department, perhaps best exemplified the type of recognition a Winona State faculty member could receive. Her Wenonah Players won acclaim throughout the upper Midwest. She received a Ford Foundation grant that allowed her to bring the cast of the Cleveland Playhouse to campus to perform Christopher Marlowe's *Dr. Faustus* and Ibsen's *Hedda Gabler*. The Wenonah Players became the first collegiate troupe to perform at the Guthrie Playhouse in the Twin Cities, putting on several sold-out performances of Ibsen's *Ghosts* with professional leading lady Judith Evelyn. Luther Gulick, the head of the Geography Department, received a Fulbright Fellowship, spent a year studying in Pakistan, and returned to campus to deliver a number of talks about East Asia. Cal Fremling won a National Science Foundation grant to study mayflies, and Fred Foss earned a College Science Improvement Grant designed to help faculty complete doctoral degrees and purchase equipment.

Other events also pointed to the growing maturity and sophistication of the campus. For the first time in 1953, the American Association of University Women (AAUW) authorized a chapter for Winona State alumnae, the first former Minnesota teachers' college to receive that distinction. The campus opened a real bookstore that sold textbooks and other materials. (Despite the faculty vote against it in 1923, the practice of renting textbooks had continued into the 1950s as part of the teachers college tradition.) Perhaps most importantly, Winona State offered its first graduate degrees, with the first master's degree recipient crossing the stage in 1954. Faculty even experimented with technology. The College of Education purchased "teaching machines" in 1962. After a student viewed a film, the machine posed a series of questions, presumably true/false or multiple choice. If the student gave the wrong answer, the machine provided the correct one, which gave the student a second opportunity to learn the material. In 1958, the faculty offered its first interactive television course, in physics no less (no doubt part of the outreach program to distant communities). Probably most faculty viewed the new medium skeptically, sharing the opinion of the nationally known speaker, Gerard Willem Van Loon, who declared that 90 percent of television programming was intended for immature individuals. Television, he predicted, would "arrest the maturity of the public at an unnaturally low level."

Despite such misgivings, the curriculum of the 1960s looked markedly different from the way it had at the turn of the century—as did the faculty, the students, the curriculum, the physical plant, and the college's traditions. In short, the college continued to maintain its social contract throughout this period by graduating teachers and liberally educated majors in diverse fields, while maintaining for the most part close and cordial relations with the community.

The Bad

In the years from 1904 to 1964, Winona State lost some of the spark that had made it great in the nineteenth century. The absence of innovation, the uninspired leadership, and a declining interest in quality, three of the five themes of the early years, constitute the "bad." During this period of mostly comfortable mediocrity, Winona State experienced some of the greatest threats to its existence. Several of these were beyond the control of the leadership, the faculty, and the community. National emergencies like wars and depression tormented all sections of American society. To their credit, presidents, faculty, students, and townspeople pulled together in these moments of crisis. Fortunately, Winona State never lacked for basic good management in this era. The bad, however, also included Winona State's slippage from national leadership to mediocrity among institutions of its type. A steady hand proved no substitute for visionary leadership and innovative thinking. Winona State became one among many; a typical state teachers' college in the upper Midwest stalled in its development. Without strong academic leadership, innovative thinking, and improving quality, the college's reputation for high standards and superb faculty eroded. In at least three of our areas of concern, then, Winona State stagnated during this sixty-year period as a result of this failure of imagination.

Wars

The two world wars and, to a lesser extent, the Korean conflict threatened Winona State with perilous times. While administration and faculty applauded enlistments as support for a worthy, patriotic cause, wars sapped enrollments, endangering the institution's finances. Gathering war clouds in Europe in 1914 slowed Maxwell's quest for a normal school in which physical activity and sports would dominate campus life. (His only academic vision, as noted earlier, was to create the best school for PE teachers in the United States.) Despite World War I's unpopularity in the Midwest, Winona Normal students and a few faculty members did their patriotic duty in the brutal trenches of France. Women also left the institution to take up jobs in industry, an earlier version of Rosie the Riveter. Despite the financial consequences and lost enrollment, Winona Normal was too well established in 1917 and 1918 to face closure as result. Nevertheless, budget crises and the general focus on international events made these years precarious for the institution. When the war ended, however, Winona Normal rebounded to its pre-1916 strength. World War II would have a greater effect and consequences.

The bombing of Pearl Harbor in 1941 profoundly altered Midwestern public opinion about the ongoing war in Europe and dramatically affected Winona State. While early on some citizens had urged US participation in the war against the Axis powers of Germany, Italy, and Japan, many others, especially in the Midwest, preferred to remain isolated. In fact, Minnesota's first citizen, Charles Lindbergh, led the charge against US intervention in World War II. Winona State reflected the mood of the region, if the campus newspaper's editorial page is good evidence, and generally ignored the brewing storm. Nevertheless, some concerned Winona State students had an interest in international events in the 1930s. First, students as early as 1931 participated in the Model League of Nations. Although the League had been formed in the aftermath of World War I as part of President Woodrow Wilson's idealistic scheme to prevent future wars, without US participation, however, it proved a paper tiger, especially in the 1930s, as the Axis powers successfully challenged its authority. For idealistic students, however, the League had great potential, so many colleges created chapters of the Model League of Nations. Winona students discussed the ramifications of current events such as the Japanese invasion of Manchuria in 1931, the Italian intervention in Ethiopia, and the question of German rearmament.

As further evidence of interest in the ongoing crisis, students formed an International Relations Club in 1933 to bring in speakers and hold discussions about the pressing problems of the day. The club debated the value of the League of Nations with some witty British students and signed a petition circulating around US campuses, encouraging the League to endorse the Kellogg-Briand Pact, a diplomatic agreement of the 1920s that formally outlawed war. One speaker talked about the Spanish Civil War, and another, a gentleman who had lived in Adolf Hitler's Germany for two years, denied reports that the Fuhrer had committed atrocities against Jews. In short, some Winona students expressed a healthy concern about the events of the day. Siding with these students, Winona State's new visionary president of the early 1940s, Dr. O. Myking Mehus (about whom much more later), called for an effective world organization once the European war ended.

After the worldwide conflict began, Winona State made its small contribution. Hitler quickly proved the importance of airpower and pummeled the French into submission. Nightly bombing shook Londoners, while brave RAF fighters and US volunteers took on Nazi pilots over the English Channel. Not coincidentally, Winona State began its aviation program at this time under Mehus's leadership, attracting eighteen men and two women the first year it opened. By the time the United States entered the war, Winona's industrial arts' curriculum included courses on Advanced Signaling and the Fundamentals of Radio. Although Winona State students became civilian rather than military pilots, they contributed to the overall war effort by relieving others to fight overseas.

When the United States formally entered the war, Dr. Mehus urged all Winona State citizens to participate in the effort by buying war stamps (US Savings Bonds) and by organizing a faculty committee for defense purposes. In addition, Mehus encouraged graduation in three years (a combination of trimming the curriculum and offering more summer classes) so graduates could replace teachers shipped overseas. In the end Mehus made quite a name for himself because of his role in the war effort, and in 1943 he accepted a position with the federal government to assist with defense preparations. (Whether this fully explains the reason for his resignation in the summer of 1943 is not totally clear, as discussed later.)

Many students and alumni fought in both the Atlantic and Pacific Theaters. During the war years the percentage of male students declined precipitously, far below the 16 percent that they had constituted in the 1920s. In fact, the class that enrolled in 1944 contained no men at all. (As a result, men's athletics were suspended.) Overall enrollments reached their lowest point since World War I, barely reaching three hundred in some years. Students no longer had to worry about getting teaching jobs after graduation, but women could find better paying and more patriotic jobs in industry. Nevertheless, as the economy boomed, the legislature did not trim the college's budget, despite lower enrollments, providing a relative funding windfall. The aftermath of the war would provide new opportunities for Winona State, especially as the GI Bill transformed the face of many institutions.

After World War II ended, international events continued to affect the public colleges in the upper Midwest. The Cold War—the standoff between the United States and the Soviet Union—heightened international tensions. Seeing itself as the defender of the Free World, the United States never fully stood down from its war footing. To protect itself and its allies from the Communist menace required the continuation of the draft; nearly all males over the age of eighteen were expected to serve at some point in the armed forces. Although men were "deferred" for certain activities, such as attending college, the draft and the deployment to Korea significantly depleted the number of men at Winona State in 1951, for example. Not all men met their military obligations via the draft. Winona State sponsored a voluntary Reserve Officers Training Corps (ROTC) program beginning in 1949. Other students met their service requirements by volunteering. Recruiters from the Navy, Air Force, and Marines regularly visited the campus throughout the 1950s and 1960s and signed students who either felt motivated patriotically or, had, for one reason or another, lost their deferments.

In the early 1950s, the Korean conflict turned the Cold War hot. The International Relations Club discussed the ongoing Korean War at length as United Nations' troops battled North Koreans and eventually Chinese back and forth across the thirty-eighth parallel. Winona State students participated in the fighting in Korea, and at least one, Rollyn Palm, gave his life in support of the US cause.

As the Korean conflict escalated, the federal government limited deferments to married men with young children and certain key professionals like doctors. Although the vast majority of young Americans, including Winona State students, were patriotic and willing to fight in the 1950s (there was none of the dissension and protests that characterized the Vietnam era), nevertheless one can detect an undercurrent of unease in student editorials of the period. Any change in draft policy brought heated responses. For example, in 1952 the Army began to require achievement tests for students to maintain their deferments, tests which fortunately Winona State students passed in large numbers. Deferred students had to be full time, score 70 percent on the test, or be in the upper half of the men in their class. Even under the more rigorous standards, most students continued to receive deferments and avoided service during the three years of the Korean conflict. Wars, however, were not the only disasters that Winona State faced.

The Great Fire of December 3, 1922

Sunday morning, December 3, 1922, dawned much like any other early winter morning in Minnesota. The temperature hovered somewhere between cold and damned cold, while a brisk north wind dropped the wind chill even lower. The college was particularly quiet, as nearly all the students and many faculty had left town on their extended Thanksgiving holidays marking the end of fall quarter. A few townspeople braved the bitter chill to take their morning constitutionals, and as one of them passed Old Main, he noticed a strange light where none should be and called in the alarm.

On Sunday morning, December 3, 1922, fire completely destroyed "Old Main," the school's only classroom building. Once again citizens of Winona and alumni rescued their school. Private organizations donated space for classes and gave money to replace lost books and lab collections. Stephen Somsen, resident director, authored a bill appropriating funds for a new building and quickly guided it through the legislature. Completed in 1924, the new structure was appropriately named Somsen Hall.

COMPLIMENTS OF
LINDSAY STUDIO

Within minutes, city firefighters arrived on the scene and initially seemed to have the blaze under control.

Suddenly two explosions erupted, rending huge holes in the building. Fire shot throughout Old Main, and flames licked at the roof. Freezing temperatures made handling the icy hoses difficult and the intense heat from Old Main prevented the crew of volunteers from approaching too closely. Meanwhile, the savagely blowing wind multiplied the firefighters' woes. Almost immediately, Winona's fire chief determined that the structure could not be saved. Shouting orders to his men, he directed their attention to the adjacent building, Ogden Hall, endangered by the spreading flames. Awakened by the clanging of bells and men's shouts, neighbors rushed outdoors and worked to prevent their own homes from catching fire. Sparks flew upwards, and the wind blew burning debris all over the city, one burning book landing as far away as Mankato Avenue at the eastern edge of town. The great fire threatened the entire community.

Meanwhile, the fire chief continued to bark orders, while his men struggled to douse the roof of Ogden Hall to prevent further damage. At last, his courageous squad won the battle. President Maxwell and concerned community members surveyed the damage. Old Main lay beyond hope of repair; its blackened outer walls stood as grim reminders of the beautiful building that had once housed the entire college's operations. Ogden's roof was soaked and badly damaged, mostly because of the firefighting efforts; eventually this would justify the demolition of the small building in 1952. Phelps Hall, upwind from the blaze, stood unscathed, as did all of the dormitories that also lay west of Old Main. Many library books had been soaked and were severely damaged. Now President Maxwell, the faculty, students and community had to decide whether this conflagration spelled the end of Winona State.

The fire united the college and the community. Some of the women students who had spent the holiday in their dorms provided refreshments to the firefighters. Faculty members penned letters thanking the crew for their hard work. In particular, the fire brought out the best in President Maxwell. Although he was a reserved man of few words, Maxwell's years of dedicated service and his strong moral principles had endeared him to the Winona community. As an active civic leader, Maxwell knew the local business and religious community well, and he turned to them in the college's hour of need. The Masons offered their temple as a classroom building and the Central Methodist Church allowed its space to serve as the assembly hall. Maxwell wrapped up these arrangements quickly and soon reported to the Board of Directors that the winter term had opened as best as could be expected under the circumstances. Once again the

Winona community had helped the college survive. But it was Stephen Somsen, the college's resident director, not the president, who made the more permanent contribution to Winona's future. Somsen had a long and distinguished twenty-four-year-career of service as trustee. He and the State Teachers' College Board persuaded the legislature to slip an appropriation for a new classroom building into the state budget. This very substantial $632,000 appropriation resulted in the construction of a new classroom and administrative building with a huge auditorium, appropriately named Somsen Hall, which opened at the beginning of the fall quarter in 1924. (It would be decorated with a gorgeous WPA mural in 1936.)

In the meantime, the state fire inspector investigated the blaze, which was deemed of suspicious origin and had cost the state a half-million-dollar-plus investment. Locals gossiped about foul play because the fire had spread so quickly and the two explosions seemed unusual. The janitor swore up and down he had locked the building when he left for the night. The fire inspector finally concluded that the explosions and the rapidly moving flames could have been caused by years of accumulated dust that had lodged above the basement ceiling, which in turn was soaked by oil used to polish the floor above. What had ignited these combustible items remained uncertain. Some speculated that faulty electrical wiring had set the materials ablaze; others favored rats playing with matches and gnawing them to create a spark. The chief reported that the building "was the worst fire trap in the city." Although the inspector could not prove it, he and others suspected arson. In addition to the suspicious circumstances of the fire itself, the inspector noted that the previous year the Mankato Teachers' College building had burned to the ground under identical circumstances (on a Sunday morning between terms). Perhaps a disgruntled former normal school student wanted revenge for some affront, or perhaps a misguided miscreant believed that along with their new designation from normal schools to state teachers' colleges the institutions deserved new structures.

Whatever the cause of the fire, the destruction of the old building marked the beginning of a new era in the college's evolution. Somsen Hall offered more modern facilities, and the crisis once again underscored the positive relationship between the community and the college. The city of Winona contributed to the library fund to rebuild the collection. Water damage had also ruined faculty gifts to the college, such as Miss Gildemeister's extensive private collection of pedagogical materials, biology professor John Holzingner's zoological collection, and the painstakingly gathered mineral collection. In response the Alumni Association called on its members to give back to the institution. Founded in 1875 by President

William Phelps, the association had remained essentially inert to this point. To celebrate the opening of the new building, the reinvigorated association convinced alumni to purchase a mechanical pipe organ from the Aolian Company to provide music during chapel (now called daily assembly) and at graduation. Although the gift arrived a little late, the organ served the college well for years. At the same time, local notables Paul Watkins and his wife, Florence, donated art purchased in Europe to beautify the building and edify students with reproductions of masterworks as they walked from class to class.

Famine

Famine also confronted Winona State. Like most institutions, the college suffered dramatically during the decade of the Depression, the 1930s. Members of the class of 1933 had no idea how their lives would change when they enrolled. The autumn term of 1929 began like most others. Most Americans believed optimistically that the prosperity of the 1920s would continue forever. Even teacher salaries had improved, especially after the newly designated teachers' colleges began promoting a four-year degree. Although by the end of October 1929, the East Coast rocked under the news of the stock market crash, this far away event meant little to the average Minnesotan. By the fall of 1931, however, the ripple effect of the Great Depression, the worst economic calamity the United States has ever faced, had reached the upper Midwest. In urban areas upwards of 40 percent unemployment became the norm, something unimaginable in the country today. Although the Depression hit urban areas hardest, its ramifications extended to Minnesota farmers as well. First, markets for products dried up, and then as part of the unusual deflationary cycle, prices fell. Farmers dumped milk and let crops rot in the field because marketing them made no economic sense. A profound economic malaise spread over the country.

As a state-supported institution, Winona State soon felt the effects of the Depression as well. Sustaining enrollment concerned President Maxwell and the faculty, but at least initially, hard economic times benefited the institution because high school graduates who otherwise might have sought employment found that avenue closed. Hence, the percentage of male enrollments increased in the early 1930s. In 1931, the college matriculated almost five hundred students, its best numbers in years. More students came from the Iron Range, the center of the depressed mining industry, than ever before. (Their US congressman was a Winona State graduate who helped recruit.) But beginning in 1933, the Depression caused enrollment to decline steadily. Only by the fall of 1938 had enrollments recovered and risen again to the mid-1931 level. Since the college traditionally depended almost entirely on enrollment driven state appropriations to survive, these enrollment declines meant revenue famines.

As the Depression worsened in the early 1930s, the state cut funding in the 1932 biennium. Voluntarily, the State Teachers' College Board requested only $2 million for 1932–33, a reduction of one-third of its appropriations. Part of the package required faculty and staff earning more than $1,200 a year to take two weeks of unpaid vacation and a 50 percent pay cut. In addition, faculty took additional reductions in successive years, only partially restored later, and in 1937 most faculty earned less than they had in 1931. On the other hand, President Maxwell did not fire any of the faculty, which he legally could have done since tenure did not exist in teachers' colleges in this era. Maxwell's gesture underscored the close-knit nature of the college community, as most faculty would have found difficulties obtaining other academic employment. Even with the reductions, by contemporary measures of income, faculty enjoyed a good standard of living. A number of them still traveled extensively in Europe and even to Asia during summers, an expensive luxury in these days before airline travel made overseas vacations practical for average citizens. System budgets stagnated for a time, and the Teachers' College Board accepted another 10 percent cut in 1940 as the effects of the lingering Depression continued. Full relief from budget woes did not come until World War II, when factories again entered full production mode.

To generate more revenue for the colleges, the Board decided in 1933 to charge tuition, a major shift in policy. From the time of Winona's founding in 1858, the institution's academic side (instructional expenses) had been provided free to all students who took "the pledge," an agreement to teach in Minnesota schools for two years after graduation. Those who refused the pledge—and this was a tiny percentage of the student body, since the curriculum focused on education—paid a fee that as of 1927 amounted to $20 per quarter. Beginning with the fall quarter of 1933, the Board charged tuition of $16 per quarter to all students in addition to the $9 activity fee, and $71 for room and board (which, as some critics pointed out, actually reduced costs to non-education majors). Out-of-state students paid an additional surcharge of approximately $2 per quarter in tuition. Even with the relatively low enrollment, Winona's tuition income added roughly $15,000 per year, including summer school dollars, to the general fund.

Increased tuition and the cost of room and board in the dormitories (estimated annual expenses in the 1930s for a year at Winona were $330) forced a high percentage of male students to work their way through college. Because of traditional gender roles in these early years, women did not have the same employment opportunities as men. In any event, expenses forced some students to abandon the dormitories to seek quarters in cheaper rooming houses and apartments near the college. Community and college benefactors alike had qualms about rising costs. As a result, beginning in the 1920s the alumni and the community provided more scholarships than they ever had before. For example, Winona businessman W. W. Norton provided an endowment from which seven scholarships were awarded annually, and when Stephen Somsen died, he left the college $10,000, some of which was used for scholarships. But these few scholarships could not offset the hardship some students faced, so the state offered another solution.

Governor Floyd B. Olsen proposed in 1934 that students be able to access some of the work relief money that the state and federal governments provided as a countermeasure to the Depression, an innovative idea that a few other progressive states soon copied. Although traditionally the federal government had largely kept its hands off the economy, the exigencies of the Depression forced Franklin D. Roosevelt and other leaders to adopt the ideas of economist John Maynard Keynes, who advocated active governmental intervention in the economy to create jobs (even make-work jobs). Such thinking required the federal government to borrow money and purposefully incur deficits, though they were small by today's standards. As the Depression deepened, the federal government offered work relief aid to create employment, supplemented in Minnesota by similar legislation. Under Governor Olsen's plan the most deserving students, forty-one at Winona, received $6 per month for expenses, with 60 percent of the money coming from federal sources and 40 percent from the state. In exchange for the money, students performed jobs on campus (buildings and grounds) or within the academic departments. Students today can thank Governor Olsen for originating the work-study program. Overall, no more than 15 percent of the student body received scholarships or financial aid, suggesting that the cost of a Winona Teachers' College education remained affordable for the middle and working class even during the Depression. Nevertheless, the squeeze of the Depression meant nearly a decade of famine for Winona State, staved off only in part by tuition and fees.

Even these relatively small sums of tuition dollars tempted those inclined to theft, resulting in the great tuition robberies of 1937 and 1938. Desperate times created desperados, some of whom like Bonnie and Clyde caught the public fancy. In 1937, some individuals operating on a much smaller scale broke into Somsen after dark and stole the collected tuition.

Embarrassed school officials confessed the next day that about $1,000 had been heisted, the remainder having been safely deposited in the bank at the close of its business day. The next year the robbers apparently expected the same easy pickings and again broke into Somsen. This time the police were prepared and foiled the robbery. A shoot-out ensued, but all of the robbers escaped. Presumably, the arrival of better times spelled the end of famine for the would be robbers as well, as this was the last such attempt on the cashier's till.

Uninspired Leadership, with One Exception

Presidents Guy Maxwell and Nels Minné managed well in moments of crisis as the previous sections explained. Nevertheless, I would contend that neither, nor interim Arthur T. French, measured up to the high standards set in the nineteenth century by John Ogden, William Phelps, Charles Morey, Irwin Shepard, and Jesse Millspaugh. The steady attrition of innovative ideas affected Winona State's regional standing, as it became merely the equivalent of all its like institutions. Despite some outstanding teachers previously mentioned, by and large many of Maxwell's faculty were inadequately prepared (which made accreditation impossible for awhile), and for that President Maxwell must assume full responsibility. In those days the president of an institution journeyed around the country and hired replacement faculty for retirements or departures. Although in his very early years Maxwell retained the Phelps-Shepard-Morey tradition of traveling to the best institutions on the East Coast to find faculty—most of whom were single women with BA's who taught only a few years—he later abandoned that practice and hired parochially. The faculty became so academically weak that the State Teachers' College Board decided in the early 1930s not to pursue accreditation throughout the system because all the state teachers' colleges would undoubtedly fail. To accentuate this point, in the 1940s, when Winona finally made the grade, the North Central Accrediting Agency stated that the "training of the staff (faculty) is adequate, but barely so." Only 15 percent had PhDs, another 55 percent MAs, and most of the rest BAs. (These credentials did not change much until the 1960s indicating that President Minné did not improve standards either.)

Faculty did not publish. When the Board asked Maxwell in 1937 to report on faculty publications and presentations, he responded, embarrassed, "Most of these items are probably less outstanding than we contemplated," and could only cite a few articles in *Grade Teacher* and presentations to Rotary. Only J. H. Sendt, an industrial arts teacher and inventor, published a nationally recognized article during the Maxwell years. Faculty thought of themselves as teachers and not professors. To be fair, faculty were very loyal to the institution and their students, and many saw this as a reasonable exchange for the lack of research and publications.

In addition, Winona's curriculum, which dated back to 1908 (and meshed with licensure requirements), looked the same as everybody else's. Electives slowly crept into the curriculum (typing, chemistry labs, social studies, and the first business courses), indicating some academic leadership on the part of the faculty. As the four-year degree became more popular, the college institutionalized half of the coursework as a general education core (then called "the commons") and the other half (ninety-six quarter credits) in major and minor courses. Students were initially required to complete two majors and one minor. In the 1930s, the "commons" became the "constants," true introductory courses. (Many course numbers will seem familiar to current students, such as Political Science 220, Psychology 220, Biology 118, etc.)

Following President Guy Maxwell's sudden death in January 1939 from pneumonia just before his planned retirement, the Board picked a very strong president, O. Myking Mehus, who had the potential to become one of Winona's greatest presidents in the tradition of William Phelps, Charles Morey, and Irwin Shepard. Coming to Winona with an earned PhD and years of teaching experience (social studies) at Northwest Missouri State, Mehus was selected because of his reputation for forward thinking. Mehus offered change for the better. Instead of singing Maxwell's tune that Winona provided "a combined general and vocational education at a smaller expense to the student than almost any other higher institution of learning," he emphasized that Winona was the oldest teachers' college west of the Mississippi, that it had nearly ten thousand graduates; a four-year curriculum, even for elementary education; a tradition of quality fine arts, especially music (Mehus' son was a violin prodigy); shop; and physical education. Thus, he placed the focus properly on academics. He encouraged new courses in the curriculum so that students "may receive a more liberal education." He even honored exemplary graduates by enrolling them in *Who's Who*.

Mehus believed that the college's academic mission came first, and he used the bully pulpit to promote the idea that higher education furthered the public good. He gave a number of speeches emphasizing the importance of education and its effect on democracy and citizenship. He lectured about the significance of service, encouraging graduates to live useful lives and to be sympathetic towards the underprivileged of every race, color, and creed. (This was heady language in the 1940s.) Year after year he toured the region, speaking about the value of education and the necessity for students of "learning the ways of democracy." As part of his very visible presence, Mehus served on North Central Accrediting teams and the National Distinguished Guests Committee of the American Legion in 1941, and worked with the Carnegie Foundation's leadership training. Mehus was one of fifteen college presidents chosen in 1939 to participate in a US Department of Education conference. In short, Mehus provided, at least for a short while, the type of vision that had characterized our nineteenth-century presidents.

To help faculty, he encouraged the teachers' college system to create the first opportunities for faculty sabbaticals, and Winona's faculty received three of the grants, all for those wishing to pursue a PhD. Mehus hired more PhDs and strongly encouraged other faculty to finish their degrees. He convinced the State Teachers' College Board to grant tenure to faculty for the first time. (All faculty had a series of one-year contracts up to the 1940s.) Mehus also maintained proudly that the student faculty ratio of eleven to one was lower than that of most private colleges. He increased the number of faculty and advocated strongly for higher faculty salaries so that Winona State would be competitive. (One faculty member before Mehus's time had left to become the principal of a high school in Rochester, apparently to get a better salary.) He converted the bachelor of teaching degree to a BS, and won accreditation for Winona State.

Perhaps the impetus for Mehus's desire to improve the quality of the institution was in response to the legislature's concerns. During the height of the Depression, several key legislators had talked about turning three of the six teachers' colleges (no names provided) into prisons, insane asylums, or reform schools, and in the 1940s they discussed the idea of eliminating the secondary education programs at the teachers' colleges to leave such training solely in the hands of the University of Minnesota. Thus, Mehus's main mission was to improve the college so that every student could "prepare himself thoroughly so he can fulfill his rightful place in bringing victory to our armed forces today and establish a just and lasting peace tomorrow."

To this end, Mehus's vision called for the construction of a number of modern facilities. His ambitious building program redirected Maxwell's priorities for athletics towards a new laboratory school and a conservatory of music. He also dreamed of a student union; the "social room" in the basement of Somsen only held fifteen people at a time. At the same time, however, he ended Tuesday Social Hour because excessive jitterbugging distracted students from their studies. He wanted athletic fields for women and agreed that the gymnasium in Phelps no longer served its purpose. He acquired Bluffside Park where he supervised the planting of one thousand trees, and also obtained Holzinger Lodge (named for the well-known biology professor) for the college. (President Minné would later return these to the city because he did not want the college to pay for their maintenance.)

Energetic, ambitious, and purposeful, Mehus got into trouble with the faculty because his reforms rocked the staid campus. Taking two rather amorphous entities—elementary education and everybody else—he created seven academic divisions, an academic affairs structure much in vogue across the United States in the 1930s. Comprising roughly equal numbers of faculty, the divisions were education and psychology, fine and applied arts, social science, language and literature, physical education, math and science, and music. (Again Mehus clearly favored music as a very important discipline.) Apparently most of the faculty balked at this reform, and by 1943 faculty discontent, Board concerns, and the offer of a position with the federal government combined to bring his resignation. Too much change too quickly seems to have undermined what otherwise appeared to be an excellent presidency.

Following Arthur French's second brief interim presidency, the State Teachers' College Board selected Dr. Nels Minné as Winona's next president. With a degree in chemistry from the University of Wisconsin, Minné possessed strong credentials, yet his many years as a faculty member at Winona comforted those upset by Mehus's reforms. Minné did indeed bring stability over the next twenty-three years as Winona State began to grow. By now, many of the old-guard faculty who had been the core of the institution in the Maxwell years had retired or died. Mr. J. H. Sendt died unexpectedly after twenty-six years of service; in addition to his inventions and his award-winning article, he had been Winona's first basketball coach (though the team lost its first game to Fountain City High School by a score of 72 to 12). Theda Gildemeister, who taught summer school at Columbia, led the fight for teachers' pensions in Minnesota. She also authored Minnesota's basic "course of study" in elementary schools and retired at age sixty-five to take care of her mother in Illinois. Louise Sutherland and Dean Florence Richards also reached the mandatory retirement age. Erwin Selle, author of the second Winona State history book, retired because of illness, as did William Munson who had served for over forty years in the model school. New faces replaced the veterans.

Although Winona State made some progress during the twenty-three-year presidency of Dr. Minné, the college did not return to its glory days, in part because of the president's limited vision. Minné explored only two initiatives during his long tenure. As a faculty member Minné initiated Science Day, an attempt to interest southeast Minnesota in the doings at

Winona State, showcasing new equipment and interesting experiments, and drawing upwards of two thousand visitors to campus. By the mid-1950s Science Day had morphed into the Science Fair, which encouraged high school students to pursue science, especially furthered by both the opening of the new science building (Pasteur Hall) and the national emphasis on science education aroused by the Sputnik scare in 1956.

His second initiative grew out of his Norwegian heritage and a Fulbright grant he received in 1949. Because of his knowledge of Norwegian, President Minné took a leave to attend the teachers' college in Oslo. His contacts there led to Winona State's first important faculty exchange and study abroad programs. Initially, Oslo Teachers' College sent a faculty member who spent two years in Winona. Then Amanda Aarestad, a senior member of the education faculty, spent a year in Oslo. Soon two, three, then four Norwegian students came to Winona State for the academic year. To drum up interest in the program, *The Winonan* published an edition in Norwegian. Winona students corresponded with Norwegian pen pals at the Oslo college, and the biology clubs at the respective institutions exchanged plant samples. To prepare students for Oslo, Winona State began offering Norwegian and Swedish courses in 1961. Because of the president's interest, the exchange program received extensive publicity, quite out of proportion to the number of students involved. Nevertheless, the Norwegian exchange began the study abroad initiative and endeared the college to the community, which respected its own Norwegian pioneers as well.

Eventually, however, President Minné fell from grace in 1966. Perhaps in part his downfall ultimately resulted from his rather autocratic administration. His fiscal conservatism, returning unspent monies to the State College Board every year, now looked old-fashioned. Although the president theoretically governed with the assistance of the Administrative Council, this body had evolved into little more than a discussion group. By the end of his presidency, faculty had written a constitution for their own governance and got it approved, despite attempts by Minné to undermine the process. Students were demanding more opportunity to speak freely in class, a hint that the college's old ways of doing business were about to come under fire. Both faculty and students now had their own senates, although the Faculty Senate was still chaired by the vice president for academic affairs. Underpaying four respected senior women faculty did not help his tenure either, and coupled with other claims of mismanagement, came to the attention of the State College Board of Trustees. As a result, President Minné decided to tender his resignation, although some sources suggest that in fact the Board outright fired him.

The Ugly: Race and Gender Issues

During the decades under discussion, attitudes about race and gender were treated in ways that later generations would find distressing, yet Winona State was neither better nor worse than other colleges facing these questions. Attitudes and experiences formed in these years are critical to understanding the 1960s and 1970s, the subject of the next chapter. Viewed through a twenty-first-century lens, some of the practices of the college in earlier decades seem downright ugly. It would be easy to skip over these topics and discuss less-controversial issues, like the football team and the oddities of the curriculum. Nevertheless, these themes are important to the social and cultural history of both the United States and Minnesota, and they existed on all campuses, not just Winona State. Thinking dispassionately about race and gender requires an understanding of the times and the prevalent attitudes of these years, not to condone them, but to bring greater understanding of earlier generations. Sometimes seemingly racist events were attempts (however misguided) to gain a deeper understanding of different cultures.

For example, clubs and student organizations loved minstrel shows in the 1920s. Popular across the nation, minstrel shows, where white performers put on blackface (black makeup), sang African-American music, usually spirituals or other popular tunes, and performed African-American dances, were attempts to make a different culture available to a white audience. At the same time, of course, these events promoted racist stereotypes. One such event in 1923, brought "colored folk from neighboring villages (who) came on foot" to hear the band. (There were clearly African-Americans in or near Winona at the time—three belonged to the construction crew that built Somsen.) Sometimes students dressed as blackfaced sailors. In the largest such show, Die-No-Mo enlisted sixty-five students to make up as "darkies," as well as Professor Theda Gildemeister, who starred as Aunt Jemima. Contemporary accounts described the show as "beautiful and graceful." More shameful by today's standards, in 1928 the annual carnival's most popular game was called "Hit the Nigger Babies," where contestants threw balls at large black dolls and tried to knock them over to win a prize. In the same decade a chapter of the Ku Klux Klan existed in Winona. The school paper records that one evening the women from Shepard Hall went over to the third floor of Morey to watch a cross burning ("a weird sight") on Garvin Heights. Better cultural understanding occurred when actual African-American entertainers performed at Winona State. The Cotton Blossom Singers held several concerts in

Somsen Auditorium, as did the Fisk University Jubilee Singers. The latter helped to maintain the connection between Winona State and that superb historically black university, whose first president had been Normal's own John Ogden. In 1932 Countee Cullen delivered a talk on contemporary African-American poets and read some of his own work.

Not surprisingly, the musical series also brought Native-Americans to campus. Chief Silver Tongue, a singer, gave the first Native-American performance, followed by Chief Ho-To-P, nicknamed "The Indian Caruso." The latter not only sang opera and Indian songs, but wore Native-American clothing and talked about his people's customs and lore. Chief Eagle Wing and his wife, Ramona, discussed customs and crafts from California, and demonstrated dance steps as well. Hopefully, Winona State students also learned from the one Native-American student known to have enrolled at the college, a Winnebago who earned her degree in 1941.

Less numerous minorities also received attention. For many summers, various rabbis came to talk to students, sometimes about the Talmud and Jewish theology and on other occasions about the social message of the Bible and Jewish poetry. Although Winona's Jewish population must have been very small in those days, the students, most of whom remained pretty religious from all accounts, were interested in learning more about the Judeo-Christian tradition. Interest in Asia was much more tenuous. In the 1920s students enjoyed the occasional "Oriental" dinner with chow mein and tea, but most of the on-campus discussion about the Asian world resulted from interviews and interactions with international students. European ethnic stereotypes also prevailed. Work crews building Somsen were described mainly as Scots and Irish, with Italians doing the marble work and Poles cleaning up the debris.

As a further aid to multicultural understanding, the college did enroll its first international students. The first such student came from France in 1923 and thoroughly enjoyed Winona. Within a decade, the college had a French club, *Le Cercle Francais,* with almost forty active members doing plays and skits. A decade later a Dutch student reported that after her family's humiliating experience at Ellis Island, Winona was a breath of fresh air. Serendipity rather than systematic recruiting brought international students to Winona. If one international student arrived and had a positive experience, not surprisingly the good word spread at home and others followed. Soon a regular contingent enrolled from the Philippines and Panama, both, of which were US protectorates during these years. The town of Quetzaltenango, Guatemala, sent four students to Winona State in 1942. These international students gave talks or granted interviews to the school paper. One student from India talked at length about his country and its leader, Mahatma Gandhi, and as a result was held up in the school newspaper as an example of the "fine strides an Oriental can make in learning the customs of the Western world." (The editor of the school paper probably did not understand that this student's British education made him more "Western" than the editor himself.) In addition, a faculty exchange program, begun during World War II with the University of Costa Rica, further broadened internationalism. In short, during the decades in question Winona State students experienced some cultural understanding of United States ethnic minorities as well as international students, even though such understandings often seem tinged with racism and a jingoistic sense of superiority.

Gender occasionally became an issue in these years, although no radical feminists populated the campus. During the 1920s, 1930s, and 1940s, women comprised between 67 and 84 percent of the student population and perhaps even higher percentages during the war years. The idea of *in loco parentis* prevailed on campus. For example, in the 1920s and 1930s, when automobiles were scarce and groups of students piled into one car to ride to dances, Miss Gildemeister made certain that the boys placed phonebooks on their laps before the girls sat down, to prevent excessive anatomical familiarity. As evidence of their second-class status, women were relegated to intramural sports. Field hockey, lacrosse, and soccer dominated the fall sports scene, while basketball provided exercise in the winter. During the spring, the women played the so-called minor sports (tennis, golf, archery) as well as "kittenball," apparently an early name for softball. With Maxwell's blessing in the 1920s, the slogan for Winona became "Athletics for All," so that women were encouraged to participate in intramural sports. Shuffleboard, ping-pong, badminton, volleyball, folk dancing, clogging, and interpretive dance widened the offerings for women's extracurricular activities. (There was a debate as to whether these should be called "co-curricular" even in the 1930s.) While the men's teams (football, basketball, and track) received huge play in the yearbook, the women's teams rarely received a single page of coverage. To showcase women's sports, there was a special section in the campus paper, condescendingly called "Squaw Talk." In short, Winona State provided a good argument for Title IX, which mandated equality for women's sports in the 1970s.

Female students on rare occasion raised questions about their role on campus. Opinion letters questioned the scarcity of women in leadership roles across the campus. Despite women's overwhelming numbers, all the class presidents and vice presidents were male (with very rare exceptions), as were the leaders of most of the student organizations. Because of male domination, the Representative Council (the name of student government until 1958) also took a very masculine point of view. Despite some powerful women in the faculty and administration (Miss Richards and Miss Gildemeister in particular; the registrar, Helen Pritchard, apparently a formidable woman; and "Mother" Potter, the de facto director of housing) and the fact that a majority of faculty were female, men dominated the institution. In fact, within the faculty ranks the college's accepted policy, consistent with national practices, paid male faculty members more than women. Male graduates received similar benefits because secondary teachers, overwhelmingly male, began with salaries of $1,500 annually, compared to female rural grammar school teachers, who earned as little as $400 a year.

Besides recognizing the unfairness of unequal pay, Winona State's women expressed their interest in political action. Granted the vote by the Nineteenth Amendment in 1920, women began to organize through a national organization called the League of Women Voters. By 1926, the League sent a speaker to talk to interested women about the "need for intelligent citizenship." The local LWV became quite active, registering women to vote and discussing the salient issues of the day. Soon a College Women's Club emerged, and by the late 1930s Winona's women played a role in the state Women's Student Government Association meeting, where they discussed issues like women's extracurricular activities, the need for more vocational guidance, and better student-faculty relations. Women were now officially referred to as "co-eds," a label that would stick until the 1970s.

At the same time, the social role of women changed as well. Women wanted more independence and fewer regulations. The age of the flapper in the 1920s promoted a more open view of sexuality, and some of the Victorian mores in place during the founding years of the college no longer sat well with the students. For example, the idea of school functions and dances ending at 10:00 or 10:30 p.m. seemed old-fashioned and, as mentioned earlier, led to barhopping downtown. To the shock of the older generation, in 1929 the college invited a woman from Boston (Radcliffe-educated with an MD from Johns Hopkins) to give a talk on sex education. "The day of the chaperone is past," Edith Hale Swift announced, which must have surprised some of her audience. More open sexuality was also evidenced with the proud announcement that one of Winona's co-eds had been chosen as the "pin-up" for the Marines Fourth Assault Company during World War II.

Although very distinct from these deeper social issues, any discussion of the "ugly" must incorporate the campus architecture of the 1950s, 1960s, and 1970s. As the legislature faced demands for massive construction projects to meet the post–World War II enrollment boom on campuses, the solution seemed to be to build unimaginative, tacky, but functional boxes. No doubt the lack of inspired local leadership did not help. Winona received more than its share of such structures, although how an architect could have designed Howell Hall without blushing remains a mystery. Aesthetics clearly remained a minor concern in the age of strict functionalism, and as a consequence, Winona State resembled many other hastily built urban campuses, crisscrossed with streets, parking lots and nonfunctional spaces. Nobody from the 1960s would have described Winona as an attractive campus. Yet like the moral blemishes, the physical warts would be covered up under later, more aesthetically enlightened administrations.

The Ozzie and Harriet Generation

At no time in its history has America seemed more secure in its values than during the post–World War II generation. Those members of the "greatest generation" and their pre-baby-boom children confidently expressed America's values, a certainty that the Vietnam era would shake. Nothing better epitomized the 1950s than the TV show *Ozzie and Harriet*, which presented the Nelson family as the ideal. The husband worked hard at a successful profession and, when home from the office, cheerily dispensed wisdom while smoking his pipe. The wife found fulfillment in domesticity, cooking, cleaning, and imparting religion and sound values to her children. The boys, while mischievous at times, studied hard, did chores, and learned valuable life lessons on their way to manhood. These stereotypical roles found their way onto college campuses like Winona State. Yet at the same time, there were gentle hints that gender boundaries were not as rigid as television fiction suggested.

During the Ozzie and Harriet generation, freshman memorized the *Beanie Booklet*, a pocket edition that summarized the institution's history, mapped out classrooms in buildings, and provided a directory of students and local businesses. Toned-down hazing still included pushing peanuts across a floor as well as diving into downtown dumpsters for tin cans, scrubbing steps with a toothbrush, and demanding students to "button up"—to raise their arms high in the air exposing their belly buttons (in the days before midriff baring became fashionable). Not all of the orientation activities were punishments; freshmen enjoyed dances and various outdoor activities as well. In some years the new students submitted to a "capping ceremony," where they held their beanies over their hearts, swore to uphold Winona State traditions and the football team, promised to show proper

Until the late 1950s freshmen were required to wear beanies during Orientation Week and forced to submit to mild hazing. That changed when the Korean War veterans and other nontraditional students began to arrive on campus. These older freshmen had no patience for "schoolboy pranks." They simply refused to participate in these traditions. Orientation shifted to an event designed to "work with" the freshmen rather than to "work on" them.

respect for upperclassmen, and pledged "to work for an attitude of community cooperation here at Winona State."

But Korean War veterans and nontraditional students had little patience for what they regarded as childish schoolboy pranks. First-year students noticeably cooled in their ardor for the ritual of passage. A pregame pep rally, usually required for first-year students, drew only three spectators in addition to the cheerleaders and the team by the late 1950s, and Die-No-Mo essentially went out of business. The near demise of the orientation program called for radical reform measures. By 1957, the New Student Orientation Team vowed to work *with* the freshmen to build school spirit, not to work *on* them. Now orientation began with Convocation and a welcome address delivered by President Minné. During the year celebrating Winona State's centennial, nearly one thousand people attended the Convocation. Freshmen wore their beanies only during the week before Homecoming, and hazing was limited to the harmless "buttoning-up" requirement—with a few exceptions, like cutting in the cafeteria line and requiring new students to call upperclassmen "sir" or "ma'am." Under more pressure, the Orientation Team discarded beanies in favor of purple and white chevrons (badges) in 1962, and set up team competitions for prizes to encourage participation in orientation.

In the 1950s and early 1960s chosen professions clearly separated genders. Women taught in elementary schools, while men chose the more specialized secondary education subjects and became principals. Generally shying away from the hard sciences, women favored the nursing program while males dominated the business courses that emerged in the 1950s. Likewise, the collegiate sports scene continued to demonstrate the division of the sexes. Baseball, football, basketball, cross-country, wrestling, and a host of other intercollegiate sports welcomed interested male athletes. While the school still boasted "a girl for every sport and a sport for every girl," women had no opportunity to compete in intercollegiate athletics. Although women did participate in intramural sports, they played a subordinate role.

Specifically, women were expected to cheer the men on as they endeavored to win league championships for the Warriors. In the days when Die-No-Mo existed, cheerleaders joined the club. As the college grew, it sought a new venue for attractive and athletic women to cheer. The new club that emerged in 1958 received the name "Warriorettes," and it soon outshone the other pep organizations. Doing dances and precision drills, the Warriorettes put on impressive half-time shows. Within two years large numbers of "co-eds" joined the Warriorettes, assuming their sanctioned role of applauding the male heroes on the athletic field.

Women also served as models of beauty and decorum. The 1950s and 1960s brought forth a multitude of queens-for-a-weekend, with nearly every major school function calling for the crowning of a queen, be it Homecoming, Winter Carnival, Freshman Orientation, or the highly competitive campus Cover Girl contest. Students expected their royalty to exercise actual duties. The victorious Homecoming Queen in 1953 touched off a controversy because as an off-campus student, she might not be always available to represent the college at certain events. The Winona State Cover Girl competed with college women elsewhere in the Upper Midwest contest. (Presumably there was a national contest as well, but no Winona State student ever advanced beyond the regional.) Marie Miller exemplified the campus-queen era. Crowned Miss Snowflake at the Winter Carnival in 1956, she went on to become Miss Minnesota. Although she did not advance very far in the Atlantic City pageant, Miller happily described her experience and the thrill of receiving a $100 scholarship for having made it to the nationals. Beauty and poise were desirable traits for the times, and Winona State women were expected to embrace these values.

The development of national sororities and fraternities underscored traditional values. In 1959, several men organized the first fraternity and applied for a national charter. After Sigma Tau Gamma selected its first forty-five members, other students formed a chapter of Tau Kappa Epsilon. To test campus sentiment about the developing Greek system, the student newspaper polled its constituents and found that Winona State students strongly favored the development of fraternities and sororities. By 1962, a chapter of Delta Zeta organized itself. This sorority proved so successful in pledging attractive young women that it dominated the campus beauty pageants. (And its members upheld very high grade point averages as well, as faculty sponsor Ruth Hopf testified.) But the coming of Greek life meant a less egalitarian social life on campus. At the same time, the popularity of fraternities and sororities reinforced the firm belief in traditional gender roles that the Greek organizations strongly encouraged.

Other evidence proving Winona State students as essentially social conservatives can be seen in their interest in religion. While undoubtedly most Winona State students had always attended church and followed their family's religions, they seemed more deeply involved with religion in the 1950s and early 1960s than students of the following decades. Perhaps students simply wanted the security of belonging to an organization in a world threatened by nuclear destruction. In any event religious clubs proliferated on campus. Beginning with the "Congo" (Congregationalists) and Wesley (Methodist) Clubs in 1948, soon the Newman Club (Catholic),

Intercollegiate athletics offered few opportunities for women students prior to the 1970s. As with most colleges and universities, women were expected to be content with intramural sports and with cheering on the men. But social changes in the late 1960s would shake up the "Ozzie and Harriet generation" and bring greater gender equality to campuses across the country.

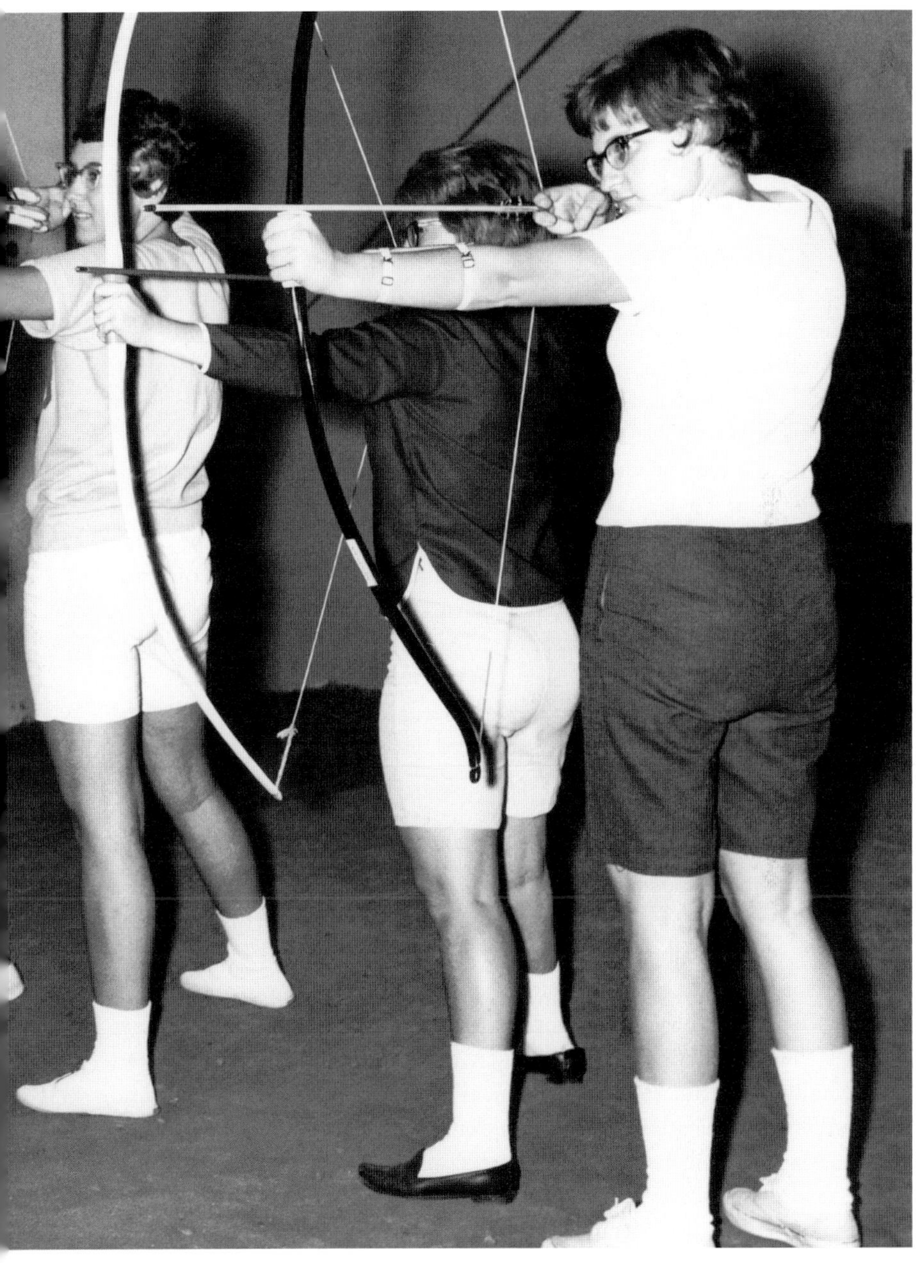

the LSA Club (Lutheran), the Inter-Varsity Christian Fellowship, the Canterbury Club (Episcopalian), the Westminster Club (Presbyterian), the C Club (Baptist), and the Bradford Club (Congregationalist and Presbyterian) came to the forefront. Pictures of the religious clubs fill the campus annuals in these years, indicating the importance of formal religion to the majority of Winona State students. Students put on the first Christmas pageant in 1964, featuring the nativity scene and the coming of Jesus. Nevertheless, the clubs had their critics. By scheduling their meetings on Thursday evenings, officially designated "Religious Night," the clubs interfered with intramural athletic scheduling and theater and musical rehearsals. Nevertheless, administrators and students retained the Thursday schedule, despite some suggestions that Religious Night be moved to Sunday.

In the same vein, students supported the idea of Religious Emphasis Week in 1959. Each January the administration set aside a week where convocations focused on religion. Student government planned the speakers, who were supposed to serve a didactic purpose. For example, one year Religious Emphasis Week discussed ecumenism, while another year the topic featured religion as a means to achieve a greater understanding of the human condition. A third year's activities outlined the duties of a responsible student, while another year featured world religions. By the mid-1960s, attendance waned just as it had with the earlier convocations. As a result, Religious Emphasis Week ended, but its existence points to the deep religiosity of Winona State students in the 1950s and 1960s.

Ozzie, Harriet, and the Nelson boys dressed conservatively, and following suit, the campus adopted a formal dress code for classes. Back in the World War II years, the co-eds had become quite informal, wearing blue jeans at times on campus. When the men returned from service, however, co-eds started to spruce up a bit and usually put on dresses or skirts for class. Men even wore suits and ties, although often more casual wear prevailed. In any event, in the early 1960s, a faculty committee chaired by Susan Day, a physical education faculty member and later an assistant academic vice president, established a "clothing code" for campus. Women had to wear skirts, and men could not wear blue jeans, or white T-shirts. The code empowered faculty to expel inappropriately attired students from class. Students at St. Cloud State lodged a protest against the code, which drew similar criticism at Winona. Some students objected to the code because they often proceeded from the classroom to extracurricular activities; other students protested that the library was too hot, making formal wear uncomfortable. Eventually, of course, the code could not stand the test of time, but it was an interesting experiment in social engineering.

Despite the straight-laced stereotypes, sexual tensions clearly existed. Coeducational recreation proved very popular. For example, the newly opened swimming pool in Memorial Gymnasium allowed for the creation of the coeducational Dolphins Club, where men and women put on a water show for the entire campus. Other students complained about the installation of a bright light outside the entrance of Shepard Hall, which presumably curtailed the length and ardor of goodnight kisses. Overall, however, Winona State remained socially a conservative campus.

Issues that would stir the campus in the 1960s and 1970s had little resonance in the 1950s. In the wake of the Supreme Court's landmark *Brown v. Board of Education* decision ending school segregation, the editor of the school newspaper challenged his fellow students to help end discrimination across the nation. Several months later, he ran a follow-up article, complaining that he had not received a single response to his moral outcry. Winona State students had no immediate interest in a crusade that scarcely touched them. Overwhelmingly white in composition, the student body did not share the racial and cultural tensions that threatened Southern or more urban institutions. With an international student population of less than twenty out of two-thousand, and a handful of African-American students, Winona State's students ignored social issues. In fact, they doubtless argued they were race blind, because they elected a Hawaiian Homecoming Queen once and in 1963 selected an African-American to serve as vice president and secretary of the freshman class. But societal changes in the late 1960s would shake up the Ozzie and Harriet generation.

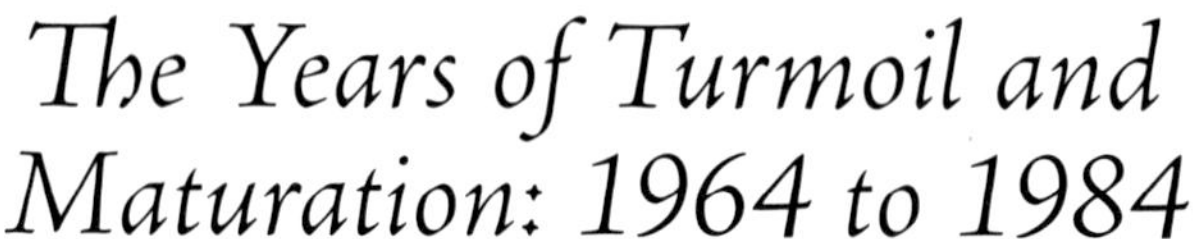

The Years of Turmoil and Maturation: 1964 to 1984

Chapter 3

The 1960s and 1970s brought great changes in American society, often caused by turmoil and ideas germinated at the nation's universities. Although Winona State's agitations scarcely rivaled activities at Berkeley or Kent State, nevertheless, students and faculty shed some of the complacency that had characterized the previous half-century, and they shared many of the same new ideas. Most obviously, the war in Vietnam provoked opposition, especially because of the threat of being drafted for combat duty, as a new generation questioned the beliefs of their parents and grandparents. Civil rights issues burned in the minds of many, who sought to rectify the injustices that had limited opportunities for African-Americans since the end of the Civil War. Other minorities (women, Native Americans) also had their champions on campuses, and social progressives made strong cases for equality. Without a doubt these causes inalterably changed the face of the university, and, in many ways, the students of these decades would find their forebearers' activities irrelevant or socially irresponsible.

While changing mores and social values marked the most important contributions of the era nationally, more modest circumstances transformed Winona State locally. Rapidly increasing enrollment during the 1960s brought greater funding and a continuation of the construction projects that had transformed the campus. Students demanded new courses, as Winona State became less defined as a teacher-training institution and more accepted as a comprehensive university with a liberal arts and sciences core. Even graduate programs flourished, as the need for advanced education manifested itself regionally and the school achieved university status. By 1984, Winona State University had changed its appearance and its mission, looking more like it does in 2007.

While in many respects, the story of change at Winona State during the 1960s and 1970s does not seem to differ dramatically from that experienced by similar institutions in these decades, the challenges of the early 1980s, set it apart and threatened its very existence. Political meddlers talked briefly of closing its doors and relocating Winona State to nearby Rochester with its large entrepreneurs, the Mayo Clinic and IBM, to serve their needs better. Coupled with that external challenge, the university also had to contend with two of the most inept administrations in its history, which created an atmosphere of distrust among faculty and support staff. Fostering turmoil and destructiveness for no apparent purpose (the declining enrollment that allegedly justified all the reforms never really materialized here) damaged Winona State and caused it to lose its way temporarily. The five themes that characterized the institution in the nineteenth-century—leadership, innovation, quality, serving the public good, and partnering with the city—fluctuated and at times disappeared entirely. Sometimes, it seems, things have to get worse before they can improve. Fortunately, in 1984 the State University Board (SUB) appointed a president who began the healing process—although decades later some of the old guard still harbored feelings of distrust. Unionization no doubt contributed to the hardening lines between faculty and administrators, but unwise administrative choices seemed at the heart of the matter.

All in all, these two decades proved the most transformational in all of the institution's development to this time. The traditions that made Winona unique were challenged and in some cases destroyed. At times people questioned whether the university still served the public good. Relations with the community frazzled, yet these decades brought about fewer changes than are sometimes attributed to them. As an essentially conservative institution located in a socially conservative part of the country, by Berkeley standards Winona remained quite traditional in most respects. If some students and faculty engaged in the national social and political issues, the vast majority remained content to pursue their degrees and future employment as had earlier generations. In other words, those participating in the great changes described in this chapter represented a relatively small proportion of the university community. Whether one was an activist or not, this era was an exciting time to attend Winona State, and it all began with the demise of the longstanding administration of President Nels Minné and the arrival of President Robert DuFresne on campus.

The Arrival of President DuFresne

By the mid-1960s, President Minné had held office for over twenty years, during which time the size of Winona State had dramatically increased, from fewer than five hundred students to well over four thousand. And, as Robert DuFresne has noted in his history of the institution, the new faculty hired in the 1960s held different expectations as to how the college should be managed. The traditional system, where the president and his academic dean made all decisions after superficial consultation with a mixed faculty-student-administrative council no longer seemed appropriate in a world trumpeting democracy and the right of all citizens to vote. (The Voting Rights Act of 1964, which swept away obstacles to suffrage encountered by African-Americans and other minorities, embodied this principle at the national level.) The new faculty embraced the principle of "shared governance" as defined by the American Association of University Professors and demanded a greater voice for the Faculty Senate. In addition, faculty called for equal pay for some experienced longtime female faculty members. Minné resisted, and soon State College Board members became embroiled in the controversy.

By late winter 1966, news filtered back to campus that the contracts of President Minné and Vice President Marion "Ray" Raymond had not been renewed. Immediately, the Board commenced a search for new leadership. Ironically, while one member of the Board reported that the reason for the president's dismissal was that he had not granted the faculty enough influence, at the same time the Board resisted having a local search committee and chose the president itself, with little campus input! In his letter of resignation President Minné asked leave to return to his teaching position in chemistry, in which he served until 1970. (Dr. Raymond continued to teach until 1974, and both men lived well into the 1990s.) The departure of Minné surprised many of the old guard who had known and worked with him for decades. For the newer faculty, however, the change in presidents demonstrated their influence. During the 1970s and the 1980s these young faculty provided the leadership that helped the institution survive its toughest challenges since the coming of World War II.

Meanwhile, the search committee recommended a new president, Dr. Robert DuFresne. With a background in education administration, DuFresne had served as a department chair at Mankato State and had long ties with the state of Minnesota. He would serve for a full decade and resolve many of the conflicts that embroiled the institution. Although he would have his critics over the decade (some would argue he dealt too leniently with protesters), he held the campus together in an era when it was not easy to do so. Arguably he presided over the most interesting period in the institution's history, as great changes, both social and political, rumbled on the horizon.

The Vietnam Conflict

Seldom has an event so defined a generation as the Vietnam War shaped the students who matriculated in the 1960s and 1970s. Not since the Civil War had an issue like this divided families and friends; heated discussions rent dining room tables and dormitory rooms. Winona State's experiences with the Vietnam era reflected the national conversation, and as at most Midwestern campuses, the tone proved more moderate and less shrill than the hotbeds of agitation elsewhere. In addition, sentiment about Vietnam changed over time, as people originally in support of their government's policies gradually turned against the escalation of the conflict. The spirited discussions, sit-ins, and occasional marches wrenched the campus from its "apathy," or perhaps more fairly stated, its overriding attention to the pursuit of credentials. More than any other generation of college students, the graduates of the 1960s and 1970s seized the opportunity to question basic American values and, utilizing the critical analysis skills they learned in the classroom, strove to create a better society.

As at most of the regional state universities, sentiment on the campus originally favored the war. In fact, the first Vietnam demonstrators on campus in the fall of 1965 marched in support of the war. Students and other interested citizens walked from St. Mary's College to the College of St. Teresa, then to Winona State and the Post Office, voicing patriotic sentiments. The Radio Club offered to send free messages from family and friends to those serving in Vietnam. In these early days President Lyndon Johnson's policy seemed to make sense: the United States had to halt the spread of Communism in Southeast Asia, and the prevailing "domino theory" held that if one nation fell to the evil Red Empire, others would soon follow, thus imperiling both the United States' closest ally in the region, Japan, and the area's newest democracy, Indonesia. But as the once token American presence in Southeast Asia grew by the thousands with no signs of victory, more and more students questioned the wisdom of our government's policy.

What provoked so many students, besides the abstract theory of our involvement and the morality of war in general, was the distinct concern that they might personally and unwillingly become part of the action. First, the enemy proved tenacious, willing to die for their freedom, and the easy victory Americans early assumed did not come to pass. Second, as casualties mounted and policymakers saw the need for more soldiers, college students feared that their deferred status under the Selective Service Act might come to an end. As mentioned in the previous chapter, under the terms of this legislation, men between the ages of eighteen and thirty-five were eligible to be inducted into the armed forces, but select groups enjoyed deferments, including college students (as well as conscientious objectors, married fathers, and others). As the need for manpower increased, students worried they might be the next to go. For example, in the spring of 1966, Winona State students heard the rumor that men with low GPAs might be drafted for the war. Others worried about financial aid, because in those days funding was tied to the Defense Department through National Defense Student Loans which meant active duty service upon graduation. By early 1967, campus editorials called for a fairer draft policy such as a lottery system, which President Richard Nixon would ultimately implement. In addition, activists called for alternative service options, such as the Peace Corps, Vista, or other volunteer organizations, which unfortunately the reformers never endorsed.

Although the student paper early in 1967 decried the campus's lack of involvement in the national protest movement, by the start of the next school year, students organized a vigil for peace. When the Army came on campus to recruit new volunteers, many protested their presence. Events took an even more radical turn when a few students, energized by outsiders, organized a chapter of the Students for a Democratic Society (SDS). Despite the rather innocuous name, this organization militantly advocated bringing an end to the US involvement in Vietnam. The Winona chapter had little self-sustaining support (their largest meeting drew only about fifty participants) and never sided with the radical fringe group, the Weathermen. Within a year or two, it disbanded because of internal dissension and external pressure. Because the SDS caused widespread civil disobedience on other campuses, including violent protests and bombings at the University of Wisconsin–Madison, the FBI also showed interest in the local organization and came to Winona to investigate our chapter. The administration willingly handed over their students' records to the authorities, which in turn triggered a mild protest that privacy issues would be so cavalierly ignored. Although the FBI investigation did affect the local SDS, other, more traditional protests escalated as the war intensified.

By the fall of 1968, peaceful protests and demonstrations became a normal, if not routine, occurrence. Protestors organized a peace demonstration and marched in support of National Mobilization Week. Brother Basil O'Leary came to campus and delivered a lecture on civil disobedience, a protest measure that gained popularity as the peace movement advanced. The major political parties offered voters a tepid choice between Hubert Humphrey and Richard Nixon, neither popular with the antiwar movement. Senator Eugene McCarthy, the frustrated senator from Minnesota, clearly remained the popular favorite, particularly on college campuses, but behind closed doors, Democratic politicians deprived him of the presidential nomination. Four years later, with Vietnam still raging, Senator McCarthy drew one of the largest crowds ever, some twelve hundred strong, to Somsen Auditorium to hear his antiwar message. The political stalemate meant that for four additional years the debate continued to rage.

Both students and faculty added their voices to the national outcry for peace (with or without honor). A freshman burned his draft card, and in an interview stated he had his parents' support for his action. Like many of his colleagues, he claimed to be a conscientious objector to the war, although he could not meet the rigid criteria that his draft board established. Professors Emilio DeGrazia and Seymour Byman helped to organize a Vietnam moratorium discussion, as well as a series of protest marches. War veterans added their voices to the antiwar fray, although the campus always contained a contingent of prowar activists as well. In short, to this point Winona State displayed rather typical and rather responsible reaction to the events going forward half a world away.

National policymakers, however, refused to relinquish the idea that the war could be won. President Nixon escalated the conflict into Cambodia, arguing that the North Vietnamese and Viet Cong resupplied themselves through their neighbor. Bombs and napalm only made matters worse, and the US antiwar movement ratcheted up the rhetoric once the news of the Cambodian invasion reached our shores. What a frustrating moment for the antiwar movement! After years of hard work wooing public opinion to its course, the "establishment" had ignored the clear wishes of the American people. Winona State reacted with the same sense of outrage as had the rest of the nation. Students declared a strike on May 6 and 7, 1970, although President DuFresne refused officially to close school. The Student Senate, led by its president, Rick Kruger, later a Minnesota state legislator, passed a resolution condemning the Cambodian invasion. By the next fall, campus bomb threats became rather routine, although investigators would never determine whether these events were linked to protests against the war.

The last major event the antiwar movement sponsored was in support of the National Day of Concern in May of 1972. Students and others wanted to memorialize the second anniversary of the Kent State shootings by declaring a strike for May 4. The Student Mobilization Committee got a healthy crowd gathered together to protest what went beyond the infringement of the right of free speech of association—the shooting of four Kent State students by the National Guard. In one last burst of energy the protesters milled around the police station and then returned to campus where they defaced the new Performing Arts Center wall with an unflattering comment about President DuFresne (which still can be seen on occasion when climatic conditions are just right). But this proved to be the swan song of the antiwar movement. By 1974, Jack Kane, the director of the Student Union, could accurately proclaim that the era of student activism had ended, and that students had returned to more traditional pursuits.

The Vietnam era, a decade of protests and change, had profound implications for Winona State. For those students involved in the movement, their activities often meant an open break with their parents and friends back home. The heady atmosphere of antiwar protests created in many a sense of idealism and an interest in committing their lives to public service (an astonishing number of student leaders from 1970s, like Tim Penny, a future US congressman, attained statewide and national political prominence). Campus values also changed. Whether in terms of interest in matters of social justice or curriculum, Winona State would never be quite the same. As a later section of the chapter will demonstrate, the curriculum would become far more oriented to the liberal arts and sciences, in part because students of this generation questioned the value of some of the professional programs (especially business) in which earlier generations had enrolled as majors. The Vietnam War caused students to think critically about other elements of life in America, and these more parochial and local reforms often concerned students more than the fight in Vietnam. Although its graduates no longer planned to become teachers exclusively, the school made good on its social contract as students filled with the sentiments of social activism and a desire to change the world spawned by the Vietnam critiques became advocates for positive change in the world. Despite all the great changes that occurred, the campus returned to its normally conservative foundations by the mid-1970s, as seen in the traditional presidential straw poll, where Gerald Ford soundly defeated Jimmy Carter (although turnout was low). The Vietnam protest, however, was just the first of the transformations that occurred in the 1960s and 1970s.

Campus Construction and Academic Changes

The decades of the 1970s and 1980s put the final touches on the physical plant that President Minné had planned. Several of the dorm reconstruction projects concluded (Prentiss-Lucas, for example) while the state experimented with a new high-rise dorm named Sheehan Hall. Although plans originally called for a matching tower, for many reasons the second building never materialized. Rumors spread that Winona's sand foundation caused Sheehan to tilt (the "Leaning Tower of Winona State"), although this story proved unfounded. More to the point, the rising water table in spring caused the basement to flood, which led to a series of makeshift repairs. Beyond that, critics noted that Sheehan towered above the city's skyline and hardly added to campus aesthetics. By the late 1970s policymakers had examined the demographics, which showed fewer high school graduates would be matriculating in college than in the baby-boom years. As a consequence, the college braced itself for a predicted decade and a half of stagnation in terms of enrollment.

Building projects also languished after the early 1970s because the recently constructed buildings seemed adequate to meet the enrollment needs of a stable campus. The final addition to Maxwell Hall gave the college a more suitable library facility to house what had become the best collection in the system, according to a consultant's report. New buildings included a new Performing Arts Center (1971) and an allegedly multifunctional classroom building named Minné Hall (1972). The Performing Arts Center gave additional space to the growing music program—too late to help Fred Heyer recruit for his band since he had tragically died. It also saw the swan song of Dorothy Magnus, who continued to direct classical plays performed by the Wenonah Players, and, in her last year, garnered a national award for her outstanding career as a director. At the same time, Vivian Fusillo opened the first run of the children's show, which has continued for well over thirty years to the present, introduced tens of thousands of students to live performances, and achieved great honors for herself as well. Otherwise, the early 1970s saw the madcap construction halt. DuFresne's request for a business-college building, the second high-rise dorm, and yet another addition to Maxwell was ignored at the state level, as was a later request for land acquisition. In fact, in 1978 the Board decreed that Winona would have no new buildings until 2000, which fortunately did not come to pass. Likewise, plans to close streets and create campus greens stagnated, as the state's investment in its higher education plants virtually ground to a halt. On the positive side, the state's unwillingness to build new edifices assisted President DuFresne's argument that the Winona campus should not be moved to Rochester, defeating that proposal in 1974.

With the state wisely holding in abeyance construction projects because of predictions of declining enrollment, the strategy for the campus administration to forestall reductions in appropriations became to chase new students. Winona proved quite successful pursuing this strategy in the late 1970s and early 1980s, being one of the few state institutions that held its own in enrollment during these troubled years. Faculty deserve much of the credit, creating innovative programs like paralegal, accounting, mass communication, and a fifth-year certificate program for high school administrators all of which piqued the interest of incoming students at the undergraduate and graduate levels. Freshmen standards, which had been a 16 ACT or top-half of one's graduating class, slipped in the name of numbers, as Winona State became essentially an open-enrollment university. Some public policy arguments helped justify this decision, as administrators claimed that institutions like Winona State were intended to provide access to all citizens of Minnesota, regardless of their abilities. For their part the faculty did try to maintain standards, as a fair number of each first-year class failed to make the grade.

In addition, President DuFresne deserves considerable credit for maintaining enrollment. He created an external studies program (now called OCED—Outreach and Continuing Education), which tapped a whole new market of nontraditional students. Through a survey, he discovered thousands of students in Winona's service area who had not completed their degrees, and by allowing them to transfer their credits to Winona State, as well as by establishing programs and hours that appealed to them, he generated hundreds of credit hours each year. DuFresne's idea of external studies no doubt saved Winona State from even worse shortfalls than will be discussed in a later section. (In many ways an organization like a college is like a shark; it must continue to swim forward and gather resources, or it will die.) Despite the stagnation of both enrollment and physical growth, faculty and administrators worked together to manage the challenge and prevent disaster. Winona's campus was sufficiently developed that it could sustain itself, and by renting dormitory rooms from the College of St. Teresa, which was struggling for survival, Winona State would guarantee sufficient housing.

New students brought other changes, four of which would become permanent. First, in 1975 the legislature, convinced by WSU faculty member and local representative M. J. "Mac" McCauley, granted university status to Winona State, along with all the other colleges in the system. After all, Winona State had been offering graduate degrees for over a decade, and similar institutions all across the country had undergone identical name changes. Second, long gone were the days when President Minné (and doubtless much of the staff) knew everybody by name. Now, each student needed to carry a photo ID, which provided access to the library, food services, and sports activities. How else could anyone recognize the more than four thousand students strolling around the campus? Larger numbers exacerbated another problem that lingers into the twenty-first century. Many students now had automobiles and insisted on bringing them to campus. By order of the Board, President Minné in 1965 established the first parking regulations and talked about the need for lots for commuters to prevent neighborhood streets from becoming congested with cars during the daylight hours. Finally, technology came—slowly—to the university. Although the last college in the system to do so, Winona purchased an

IBM machine for the Registrar's Office once enrollment numbers pushed over two thousand. One wonders if hard-nosed Miss Pritchard would have accepted this innovation? Certainly, as noted in chapter 2, President Minné resisted it. Thus, the new, larger student body had tremendous impact on services offered on campus.

Social Activism and Reform

The idealism of Vietnam-era students manifested itself in several different ways at Winona State. Whether to avoid military service or because of a genuine commitment to better the world, Winona State students flocked to service programs like the Peace Corps and VISTA. Peace Corps volunteers shipped all over the world, rendering invaluable services in Asia, Africa, and Latin America (despite suspicions of intellectuals in those regions that they were covert CIA agents). VISTA sought to improve conditions in the poorest regions of this country, like Appalachia. Recruiters for these agencies found a warm welcome on campus from the mid-1960s until the mid-1970s. Statistics do not exist to show how many volunteers from WSU went abroad in service of their country, but clearly many did so. At the same time, many idealists also believed in the value of military service in Vietnam, and their contributions should not be forgotten either.

The new idealism also manifested itself by offering students the opportunity to listen to speakers whose names became associated with the great causes of the 1960s. Included among campus speakers were the famed historian Arthur Schlesinger Jr., economists Milton Friedman and John K. Galbraith, the prize-winning poet John Ciardi, the film star Vincent Price, and the editor of *The Atlantic Monthly*, Edward Weeks, as well as Governors Karl Rolvaag and Al Quie and Senators Walter Mondale and Hubert Humphrey. Sargent Shriver came to talk to students about the Office of Economic Opportunity. Shriver, the first director of the Peace Corps, challenged students to think about helping the poor. President DuFresne urged first-year students to become more activist and to work on issues of race and morality. Dick Gregory, the comedian and civil rights activist, also spoke at Winona State, describing the experiences of African-Americans and the problems of discrimination. Florence Kennedy, a black feminist, talked about the issues facing African-American women. Students took up other challenges as well, forming a committee for Biafran relief in support of the people of that province of Nigeria suffering fearful repression in the late 1960s. Over seven hundred of the nine hundred students on the campus meal plan gave up a meal to support the Biafran cause. When the American Indian Movement (AIM) reached its apogee after the Wounded Knee protests, Russell Means and Dennis Banks lectured about the plight of Native Americans to a large, cheering audience. Their attorney, William Kunstler, made his second WSU appearance, having come once before to apprise students of the case against the Chicago Seven, the protesters arrested at the 1968 Democratic Convention in Chicago.

Of all the campus groups involved in social commentary, the Black Student Union was the most active. The group, founded in 1969, quickly recruited a significant following. Wishing to expand African-American students' (and majority students') cultural awareness, they published a weekly column in *The Winonan*, usually about a topic of black history. They tried to raise money for scholarships for African-Americans and wrote an interesting editorial suggesting that blacks ought to be exempt from the draft because of previous injustices. Two years later, the organization held a "rap session" for the campus, trying to clear up stereotypes about blacks for the white majority. They established a house at 516 West Mark Street and published a very telling piece in the college paper about the difficulty of being accepted in an all-white community as Winona essentially was in those days. In 1975 the organization changed its name to the Black Cultural Awareness Club (with Cal Winbush as its advisor) and changed its mission to include bringing black culture to the majority. They sponsored dances, keg parties, lectures and ongoing rap sessions just like other campus groups. For example, in the mid-1970s, they organized Black History Week (now part of the national Black History Month) and held a talent show and dance.

In another example of social activism, Winona State helped to support several Ethiopian students for a year when a dreadful civil war broke out in 1974 in that land. After the year, however, with no resolution in sight, the school expelled two of the Ethiopians who could not pay tuition and who refused to perform work-study jobs as had their fellow countrymen. Unwilling to return home in the midst of the chaos, these students sued the university. Years later after several hearings, the case was dismissed, although in the interim one of the students, an unsuccessful candidate for student association president, caused a considerable amount of trouble. In these activist times, the students received very sympathetic treatment from their peers. Another act of altruism came in 1965 when Winona State students participated in large numbers in response to the great Mississippi River flood. Filling and heaving sandbags, the students stood shoulder to shoulder with community members, trying to prevent a local disaster.

In short, Winona State students responded positively to the message of social activism and change that characterized the civil rights movement and other social movements of the 1960s and 1970s. Whether listening

Students in the 1960s and 1970s responded to a call for social activism. The peace movement, the civil rights movement, and a war on poverty all motivated students to action. A local crisis occurred in 1965 when the Mississippi River's spring flood reached a record crest and threatened to destroy the city. Winona State students (pictured above) and other young people in the area picked up shovels and sandbags and helped to keep the river at bay. Nearly two generations later, in 2001, WSU students again in large numbers joined in the rescue of another river town, Fountain City, Wisconsin.

ICE

to speakers, participating in activist organizations, or engaging in community activities, Winona State students partook of the social movements of the day. That they did so in the absence of a real minority community in Winona shows remarkable awareness. By 1975, the Black Cultural Awareness Club enrolled thirty members, a very respectable number. Overall, however, minorities remained a small fraction of the student population. A look at the graduating classes of 1965 and 1966, for example, reveals a single African-American and a single Hawaiian in each class, the sole minority representation. An African-American woman did become the Campus Cover Girl in 1967. A few Japanese students appeared in the late 1960s but generally the international student population remained low, as the club enlisted only fifteen members in 1971. All in all, then, the social movements of the era resonated well with the students, and like campuses all over the country, Winona participated in the new activism.

Old Traditions Die Out

The 1960s and 1970s not only brought new ideas to fruition, but they also ended many old traditions. These changes tended to reflect new values and interests of students and society. This section, then, will examine the traditions that marked the rhythm of the academic year and the rapid change that took place in them during in these two decades. At the same time Winona State's social clubs made new beginnings and new endings. In addition, as the nature of the university itself changed, so too did its curriculum. Finally, the university's administrative structure modernized itself, closely resembling today's hierarchy. Like so many similar institutions, Winona State reached adolescence as a university in the 1960s and 1970s.

The school year still began with First-Year Orientation, as it had since the 1920s. Early on a first-year student experienced the same orientation program outlined in the *Beanie Booklet* from the 1950s. In the early 1960s, all new students still wore identifying purple beanies, and orientation culminated with a formal convocation and a big dance, where a king and queen presided. By the end of the decade of the 1960s, many of the women in the class were photographed for the yearbook in jeans, and beanies had disappeared, worn only by the leaders. A few of the men had facial hair, and one character posed with a cigarette hanging out of his mouth. By the end of the 1970s, orientation had become purely a social activity, designed to integrate students by showing them the "fun side" of college, while the elected "royalty" had passed from favor. Carl Stange, currently director of admissions, was but one of the eager young student leaders who then brought a sense of excitement to the orientation program.

Homecoming, too, modified itself over time. In 1965, a nontraditional student became queen—a married woman (to the quarterback) with two children. Bonfires eventually disappeared, as did the Snake Dance around the downtown. Talent shows and concerts replaced two of the traditional dances. New Homecoming dance themes included "Gone to Pot" and "Psychedelic 67," both of which would have been unthinkable in the 1950s. Clearly the credentials for Homecoming Queen became less formal. As late as 1969, though, each candidate still wore a dress for her yearbook photograph, a practice that would soon end. By the early 1970s few women vied for the office, and Homecoming press coverage was much diminished. The pep rally, instead of being held in a huge field with a sparkling bonfire, now had such limited attendance it took place in the cafeteria. The egalitarian nature of the time revealed itself when popular history professor, Henry Hull, wrote an editorial in the school paper denouncing the idea of "royalty" as being undemocratic. For a while, apathy reigned, as many student activists thought their important causes superseded the frivolity of Homecoming.

Many of the old traditions faded in the 1960s and 1970s. Events surrounding Homecoming, Orientation, and the Spring Prom either disappeared or were greatly altered. Popular professor Henry Hull denounced Homecoming royalty as being undemocratic. However, by the early 1980s many of the traditions, like Homecoming and school dances, had staged a comeback.

By 1976, however, the event staged a comeback, which has been building thereafter. First of all, it became more acceptable to have fun in traditional ways, and secondly, Homecoming's organizers revived traditions like the Medallion Hunt, which had been discontinued for ten years. By the time the 1980s rolled around, dancing had become respectable again, and spectators remarked that the students responded more enthusiastically to the celebration. (In 1981 though, a small scandal broke when eleven men mooned the crowd at half-time of the football game with "Win-Winona" displayed on their butts.) The Hall of Fame for outstanding athletes began in 1983, creating an impetus for alums to return to honor their athletic friends and classmates. In sum, after a few years of dwindling attendance, Homecoming regained its importance as the major event of the fall semester.

The myriad dances that punctuated the school year also changed. Like Homecoming, the traditional dances held on into the 1960s, withered during the protest years, and came roaring back in the late 1970s and early 1980s. The spate of monthly dances of the 1950s continued briefly. Christmas dances, Winter Carnivals with Miss Snowflake (until the city took over the event), the Valentine Dance, and Spring Carnival each brought another occasion for the coronation of royalty. Less formal sock hops continued until the late 1960s as well. Dr. DuFresne added the President's Ball, where students not only dressed formally and danced, but enjoyed an elegant sit-down meal with such fare as prime rib and wine. (Cocktails were served off-campus before the festivities began.) At the end of his term, the event was renamed the Scholarship Ball, and perhaps more appropriately, raised proceeds for scholarships for deserving students struggling with rising costs. An editorial in 1966, which talked about the university's plan to end informal dances because they were overcrowded, demonstrated the popularity of the social events. Then came the early 1970s, when dancing lost favor with much of the college crowd. Bearded youths and blue-jean clad women swayed arhythmically to the beat of protest songs, but scorned the traditional events. By the end of the decade, for better or worse, disco came into vogue (later most people would deny they participated—yet the movement flourished) and dancing became popular again. Soon "Disco for Charity" events sprang up, allowing for wholesome fun but also generating profits for worthy causes.

The most important dance tradition also followed this see-saw of popularity. Spring Prom had been the highlight of the social year for decades, an event that many graduates remembered with great joy. Traditional themes held well into the 1960s, including "Magnolia in the Deep South" and "Spring Romance." The dance now lasted until 1:00 a.m., an unseemly hour in the eyes of elder statesmen, but a concession to the changing times. Organizers of the event still required students to wear formal dress. But the same disdain that frowned upon dancing during the protest years also took its toll on the Prom. By the mid-1970s, the annual event ended because of poor attendance and a clear lack of student interest. Traditions sometimes have a life of their own, however, especially deep-rooted ones like the Prom. And so, in 1982, a very different era, the students decided to revive the Spring Formal, as it was now named. With some fits and starts the event became a permanent part of the annual social calendar if with some important modifications. The event now happened off campus, in locations like the Holiday Inn, which also offered partygoers reduced room rates for the night.

Similar social events continued to occur as they did on all college campuses. These included events like Greek Week (which temporarily replaced the Winter Carnival), the Spring Carnival (which evolved into the Spring Frolic and later the contentious Springfest of the late 1980s and early 1990s that threatened good relations with the community because of the behavior of drunken students), and the more prosaic Parents Weekend. Fraternities and sororities sponsored many of these events, like Delta Zeta's annual fall fashion show (this may have begun as a bridal show in 1965). Showing the continuing strength of traditionalism, new fraternities and sororities, some affiliated with nationals and others not, brought more social events to campus. Greek Week included a talent show, in which faculty sometimes participated, as well as a dance and a special banquet. Parents Weekend, originally just a day, brought the folks back to campus to visit their students, fed them a fine meal, and put on some entertainment for them. In short, the "fun" social activities continued to play an important role at Winona State, albeit in light of the larger enrollment, perhaps a more tangential one. Compared to large campuses, fraternities and sororities played a relatively minor role at Winona State, where the vast majority of students remained independent. Finally, graduation, sometimes outdoors at Maxwell Field, ended the academic year just as it had since the 1860s.

For many of the students, other social outlets included sports and clubs. The major sports teams all enjoyed some successes during these decades, winning conference championships. The football team won its conference in 1965 and 1983, basketball in 1969, 1971, and 1972, and the baseball team remained a perennial powerhouse. Even Luther McCown's retirement did not stop that juggernaut, as Gary Grob went on to become the winningest coach in Winona's history. The baseball field was named for Peter Loughrey of the class of 1900, then the oldest living Winona letterman. Of the minor sports, wrestling often dominated the headlines, as the Warriors grappled successfully nationally.

For most of these years, the women engaged in club sports, at least until the coming of the 1978 federal legislation known as Title IX, which mandated equal funding for women's sports. The ensuing cuts to men's sports (the elimination of the wrestling team still rankles some alumni) allowed women to compete intercollegiately. Of all the women's teams fielded, the gymnastics squad enjoyed the greatest success. Beginning in 1982, the Warriors placed seventh nationally among small colleges and continued to improve every year through 1984, when they placed second nationally in the National Association of Intercollegiate Athletics (NAIA). The university's top gymnast, international student Sylvia Ponce, won special recognition for her abilities. Of the other activities, forensics and debate enjoyed the greatest prominence, with coach Susan Rickey Hatfield and student Victor Vieth leading WSU to several national tournaments in the 1980s (despite a scandal involving the former coach who allegedly allowed the team to drink and use pot to prepare themselves for debate competition).

Federal Title IX legislation in 1978 mandated equal funding for women's sports. Winona State's gymnastics team quickly became a national power. In 1984 the Warrior women placed second in the National Association of Intercollegiate Athletics gymnastics tournament. Over the years women's gymnastics has been one of the university's strongest athletic programs.

Social clubs offered another opportunity for WSU students to get together. Music, particularly the Concert Choir, provided cultural outlets and allowed students to travel, sometimes beyond state borders to St.Louis and even internationally to Mexico City. The Wenonah Players, the longest-standing club on campus, continued the tradition of performing classical drama, staging Sheridan's *The Rivals* and Aeschylus's *Agemememnon*. With far less frequency than in the 1930s, classical performances came to campus: the Indianapolis Symphony, the St. Paul Chamber Orchestra, the National Ballet Company, and a New York touring company that put on *La Traviata*. But audiences for these events had dwindled, making them generally impossible to afford. Because of funding problems in the 1970s, the campus radio station, KQAL, and the campus television station grew much less rapidly than hoped. Sharing the college's traditional values, the religious clubs remained popular, even through these more skeptical times when students publicly debated the question "Is God dead?" The Newman Club, the Canterbury Club, the Wesley Club, Gamma Delta (Missouri Synod), the Christian Science Club, the Lutheran Student Association, and the newest, Inter-varsity Christian Fellowship, demonstrated that religion still played an important role in the lives of many students. Although clubs as a part of campus life declined in the 1970s—at least if photographs in the yearbook are a fair indicator—one new club emerged that showed the whimsically critical attitude of the contemporary student. The Mickey Mouse Club, which held that not only was Mickey real but was the "Savior of Mankind," claimed that their organization offered an alternative to the drinking and drugs so prevalent on campuses in those days.

Most of all, these years may best be known as a time when several longstanding traditions at WSU ended. A few of these brought no tears, but in retrospect, others probably should have been retained, or perhaps should be reborn in the twenty-first century. Few today would regret the passing of the weekly assembly, which apparently met its demise in 1965. The Science Fair that the university hosted under President Minné shifted direction of Professor Fred Foss and remained an important recruiting tool. The Purple Key Society, which honored the top ten students at the university no longer existed after the early 1970s. Because of a lack of subscriptions, the college yearbook, *The Wenonah*, failed in 1972, although smaller editions were published sporadically until 1976. Phelps Model School closed in 1973, and its students entered the Winona public school or the private Catholic system. Once again, editorials blamed student apathy for the changes in campus life. But while many of the old campus traditions ended or evolved, students and their lives also changed with the times, and it is to these new concerns that his chapter turns.

Sex, Drugs, and Rock-and-Roll

The 1960s and 1970s oversaw a dramatic change in American popular culture and in this arena, the students shocked their parents. No longer would students accept the older generation's cultural norms. While classical music concerts on campus, once a regular feature, now happened only every few years, popular culture events literally took center stage. And while the earlier generations had been content to tipple a few brews in downtown bars and neck in parked cars or at the door of the girls' dormitory, the new mores permitted radical changes in behavior. Both the quantity and type of "mind-altering substances" changed. Yet the new behaviors at Winona State, shocking as they seemed to townspeople and alumni, were moderate in comparison to those on other campuses on the East and West Coasts. Nevertheless, these new attitudes were so marked and so pervasive that they merit discussion.

Alcohol had long been the drug of choice among college students, banned though its use was on campus. World War II veterans had brought with them freer attitudes toward alcohol consumption, and both local merchants and campus officials doubtless turned a blind eye when these nontraditional students quaffed a few beers. With the coming of the Vietnam era, new drugs jumped onto center stage, beginning with marijuana. According to the youth culture, smoking pot had positive benefits—no hangovers, no bloat, and a more "mellow," less belligerent high. Soon, Winona State students expressed an interest in the new drug of choice. As early as 1967, campus editorials advocated the legalization of marijuana, though not of the hallucinogen LSD. Seeking to educate and persuade, the paper also published scientific findings about marijuana. According to the graduate student scientist involved in the research, marijuana was not addictive, nor was it a sexual stimulant, nor did it lead to more serious drugs. Later evidence suggested, however, that pot was not so harmless. A survey in 1971 indicated that 6 percent of WSU students used pot regularly, 20 percent had tried it, and 1 percent had experimented with hard drugs. (At the same time 51 percent of men and 19 percent of women confessed to smoking cigarettes.) Police arrested one student for selling marijuana, and periodically school officials found pot in the dorms, although the students involved often escaped punishment on technical grounds.

At the same time, the hallucinogenic drug LSD also appeared on campus. Marketed originally as the ultimate "mind-blowing" experience, LSD "trips" became the rage on many campuses. Publicized by Harvard professor Timothy Leary, the drug became popular with musicians and then with the audiences who listened to them. Although originally thought entirely safe (Leary described at great length his many positive experiences), some began to question the drug's effects. A WSU chemistry student wrote an article talking in scientific terms about its possible harmful side effects. Nevertheless, it could be found on campus. At a party honoring a new WSU faculty member, George Bolon, a student spiked the punch with LSD, which severely affected a fellow student. As a result, the perpetrator found himself facing a one-year jail term, although the judge ultimately suspended the sentence.

While the presence of drugs marked a radical behavioral change on the part of some WSU students, for the most part the students preferred liquor. Easier to obtain, quasi-legal to possess, alcohol permeated the campus to a greater degree than ever before. A survey in 1981 reported in the school newspaper estimated that 94 percent of WSU students consumed alcohol. With this large number in mind, it is not surprising that the top social issue was whether liquor ought to be allowed on campus. The statewide student association argued that each campus could make its own rules because no state statute governed the question at that time. Soon students petitioned to have alcohol on campus, supported by many faculty, although the university presidents as a group rejected the idea, saying that alcohol was "not part of the educational process." Soon the legislature got into the act, lowering the drinking age to eighteen (if we're old enough to fight, we're old enough to vote and drink, the argument went), which made most WSU students legal consumers. Jim Pehler, later a statewide Inter-Faculty Organization (IFO) president but then a legislator from St. Cloud, several times beginning in 1979 introduced a bill to allow liquor in dorm rooms, but the bills always lost.

Although the lower drinking age met with popular approval on the part of students, its deleterious effects soon became apparent. Not all eighteen-year-olds could handle their liquor wisely, so both legislators (by increasing the drinking age in the 1980s) and school officials tried to restrict students' liquor consumption. In general, the school's philosophy encouraged controlled drinking under socially acceptable circumstances. City officials, too, got into the act by trying to limit consumption. Neighbors complained about keg parties that went on too late and loosed drunken students into the streets at all hours. As a result, the city considered banning keg parties, but in the end restricted the occasions when "keggers" could be held. Consequently, the students pressed for kegs on campus, and President DuFresne agreed. Social organizers could apply to the Ad Hoc Liquor Committee, which could then grant licenses on a limited number of occasions. Casino Night in Kryzsko Commons was very popular in the late 1970s, where students could combine blackjack, roulette, a massage parlor, and beer. Officials punished students who brought kegs on campus illegally. (For example, a freshman caught with a keg in his dorm was placed on probation in 1975.) Punishments for alcohol violations became more severe as time passed. One student leader, Jim Schmidt (now WSU's vice president for university advancement), reasonably advocated a campus pub serving 3.2 beer as a means of keeping students on campus over the weekend, but to no avail. Ultimately, the trend moved in the opposite direction, in part because the rising cost of liability insurance for the keggers made them less and less desirable for the university's administration. Along with the consumption of "recreational" drugs, the new attitudes toward drinking mirrored the permissive age that had arrived with the Vietnam protest era.

Likewise, views about sexual morality changed in these decades. One can only be amazed at the differences between the early 1960s and the 1970s. Traditional values held sway at first. A woman student in the early 1960s argued in the school newspaper against premarital sex, citing the dangers of disease and pregnancy, and ultimately basing her decision to remain a virgin on religious authority. Her article did spark a debate, showing times were changing. At first the new morality expressed itself in almost childish ways, as exemplified by the infamous "panty raid" of 1964, when men invaded a women's dorm and stole underwear as souvenirs. This particular caper was well planned for the perpetrators had disabled the phones in both Shepard and Richards and then systematically raided every room. School officials investigated the prank, caught the "villains," and disciplined them. Although the raid of 1964 seems to be the only such incident on our campus, these pranks elsewhere seemed to lose favor when women became willing co-conspirators and the shock value disappeared.

Female deportment raised lots of eyebrows as well. In the early 1960s the campus newspaper came out in favor of retaining the dress code that Professor Susan Day and a faculty committee had mandated in the 1950s. According to the campus editor, students would be served well to dress like adults. But yearbook photographs evidence the change, from portraits uniformly in dresses and skirts in the early 1960s, to the 1970s, when almost all women wore jeans. By 1968, female students complained openly about the dress code, and they ignored it. Other policies seemed old-fashioned too, and the room-check policy created ire. Some students queried the idea of restricted hours for students who were over twenty-one years of age and also for seniors, thought to be sufficiently mature to make decisions on their own. Resident Assistants issued demerits for dirty floors and sinks and messy closets. Dress-code violations and late check-ins at a dorm also resulted in demerits for women demonstrating the sexist nature of the system. Other rules included an open-door policy when someone of the opposite sex visited your room, the "four-feet on the floor at all times" regulation, and the prohibition against wearing swimsuits outdoors on campus. Too many demerits resulted in a woman being "campused"—confined to her room from 7:00 p.m. to 7:00 a.m. Within a few years, all of these policies would be questioned and revised.

That sex was on student minds became very clear when the Student Senate demanded that the Student Health Clinic provide free contraceptives. By 1970, the issue of co-ed dorms reached student consciousness. A questionnaire indicated that most students favored the notion, and the university slowly began to adapt. Fourth-floor Prentiss went co-ed in 1971, and at the same time the school abandoned parietal hours for upper-class students, while warning that the changes were only temporary. Soon Richards went co-ed, and the rest, with the exception of Sheehan, followed suit. By 1974, a mere decade from the first discussion about premarital sex in the campus newspaper, an editorial appeared from a group of women strongly opposed the idea of preserving one's virginity for marriage.

More open attitudes about sex and greater sexual activity on campus did have consequences. Although college women as a rule experienced fewer unwanted pregnancies than their age population as a whole, presumably because of their greater knowledge, at times Winona State students did become pregnant. While most of these life-altering experiences turned out well (or at least safely), in one spectacular instance it did not. In 1981 Margaret Kinsky, a paralegal student, was convicted of second-degree murder and sentenced to ten years in prison when she was found guilty of strangling her newborn infant with her bra strap in her dorm room. According to the testimony, a man searching through the dorm garbage looking for returnable cans found the baby where Kinsky had dumped her. As the story unfolded, the evidence revealed that she gave birth while her roommate slept. When prosecutors revealed that Kinsky had given birth to another illegitimate child previously and put him up for adoption, public sympathy for her eroded. An editorial stated that she received exactly the punishment she deserved, although a few letters to the editor demurred. (The only other major felony from these years was the case of a WSU accounting student accused of two bank robberies.)

The nature of WSU's ideal woman also changed over time to become more sensual. In addition to the tradition of multiple queens crowned during the year during the early 1960s, the standard beauty pageant moment came in February with the selection of the Campus Cover Girl. Chosen for a combination of beauty, charm, and activities, the Cover Girl then competed in the Upper Midwest regional contest, and then nationally, though, as noted WSU did not have any of its women advance beyond the regional competition. The Cover Girl competition originally seemed clearly aligned to the Greek system; a Delta Zeta nearly always won in the 1960s and most of the competitors one year belonged to that sorority. In 1968, however, a popular African-American woman won the contest, and the next year nearly took the Homecoming crown as well. By the early 1970s, however, the Cover Girl contest died out, replaced by another event more overtly sexual.

In the winter of 1969 the TKE (Tau Kappa Epsilon) fraternity sponsored the first of its annual Playboy Bunny candidate contests. Armed with decorations, advice, and assistance from Playboy headquarters in Chicago, the TKEs held the event in the Union, complete with a full bar, a casino, and Delta Zeta pledges dressed in bunny costumes. With the trademark ears, tails, short skirts, and tights, the bunnies served drinks and acted as hostesses for the evening. Candidates for the big prize ($500) wore miniskirts, and a panel of students and faculty (the ever-popular Henry Hull) judged the young women on appearance, personality, and admitted "fudge factors." The celebration drew a relatively small crowd (as did the "shortest skirt on campus" contest, which another fraternity thought up), but participants reported that Dining Rooms C and D were indeed lively places on those evenings. After the fifth Annual Playboy Bunny Contest in 1973, however, some women wrote the school paper asking the fraternity to discontinue the practice because it was demeaning to women. Apparently the message hit home, and these celebrations ended. By then, the new feminist movement had begun to take on other serious issues besides sexual freedom.

Equality for most women meant nondiscrimination. Editorials both pro and con flew back and forth about the Women's Liberation Movement and the use of the abbreviation "Ms.," to avoid discrimination by marital status. Others applauded the new equality offered by Title IX, a huge improvement for women's sports, even as men complained about eliminating the wrestling team. By the spring of 1978 the law had been implemented; now the university had nine men's and eight women's teams, as well as a significant women's intramural program. As time went on and people complained that the university did not spend proportionately enough money on women's sports, many alums figured that ultimately major men's sports, like football, would suffer. As a result in 1980 alums created the Warrior Club to raise private money for men's athletics, a permissible practice under the statute. Despite some specific concerns, almost everyone on campus agreed that Title IX served an important function, allowing women equal (or roughly equal, in this instance) privileges with college men.

Other issues, some minor, some important, highlighted the changes caused by the sexual revolution. Fads including body painting, streaking (the practice of running across campus in the nude—a scene caught on the new WSU television station), and toga parties (dressing in Roman togas as in the popular contemporary comedy *Animal House*) all had their season in the sun. More seriously, crimes involving sex—a shower peeper in Sheehan and Richards, a guy breaking into women's apartments and stealing underwear—made headlines and led to a sense of a greater need for security by the end of the 1970s. Downtown, the Women's Resource Center opened to provide services to battered women, and the campus began to sponsor an annual Take Back the Night event to provide greater awareness about sexual assaults.

For the first time, students also talked openly about gays in their midst. A Minneapolis organization provided information about their Gay Community Services, and an alum wrote a letter to the newspapers about his difficulties hiding in the closet during his undergraduate years. In sum, Winona State experienced the same sort of issues about sexual freedom as other college campuses around the nation.

From the parental perspective, the new openness regarding sex all resulted from the devilish sounds of rock-and-roll. And indeed popular music concerts became a major tradition in the 1960s and 1970s, as classical music lost its audience. Students looked forward to the Homecoming Concert, which featured big-name bands, although the nature of the music changed dramatically over the years. While early in the 1960s students applauded wildly the clean-cut Four Freshmen, within a couple of years they wanted protest singers like Glen Yarborough, soul singers like Peaches and Herb, or rock hitmakers like the Sandpipers, Gary Puckett and the Union Gap, Mac Davis, the Yardbirds, the Guess Who (later just the Who), the Association, and Olivia Newton-John. Big-name comedians also billed themselves at Somsen Hall: Lily Tomlin (although she said she was bored and left the stage early) and Gallagher with his smashing watermelons act. The university continued to attract big name acts throughout the 1970s: Melissa Manchester, Pure Prairie League, Charlie Daniels, Harry Chapin, the Ozark Mountain Daredevils, to name the best known.

In the 1980s, however, big-name pop concerts became a thing of the past for several reasons. When Hall and Oates cancelled in the spring of 1982, student leaders reported that the singers refused to appear because they wanted more money. Suddenly in the 1980s prices for rock concert tickets escalated, and as a result smaller venues like Winona State could not afford Top Ten groups. Lesser-name acts naturally drew fewer people. (Johnny Holm and Cheap Trick were good bands, but more regional.)

Further, now that dancing had reemerged as an activity, fewer people wanted to spend their evening sitting in Somsen listening to a band. As a result, in the spring of 1984 student officers announced the end of rock concert series because attendance had become too small. A group named Suburbs had managed to draw an audience of only six hundred, which did not make the series financially feasible. Hence, the era of big-name rock-and-roll events on campus came to an end, even though popular music remained a dominant art form in the culture.

In sum, the 1960s, 1970s, and early 1980s radically transformed the society in which Winona State students and faculty operated. Critical attitudes about the war led to a relaxation of many of the mores of traditional America, and college campuses led the demand for change. Although Winona State hardly pioneered these changes, the university did fully participate. With greater freedom came greater responsibility, which, in most instances, Winona students met well. The decades greatly changed the worldview of most Winona students and caused great consternation among more traditional faculty members. But faculty had other worries. Besides the financial crisis caused by declining student enrollments that drove funding, the faculty also had to deal with the most destructive administrations in the history of the university, which took office in the late 1970s and continued into the early 1980s. To that story we must now turn our attention.

The University in Crisis Once Again: 1975 to 1983

The university also changed in the 1970s and 1980s because of prolonged financial woes and ongoing hostility between faculty and administrators. In fact, not since the enrollment crisis caused by the coming of World War II had the college faced such a financial threat. Compounding that problem was a lack of leadership. Matters had gotten so much worse that some faculty probably pined for the certainty of the good old days of President Nels Minné. As previously mentioned, the 1960s had been a decade of growth for Winona State. Not only had the physical plant expanded, but the professoriate rapidly grew in size in order to provide classes. From a faculty of 118 in the fall of 1964, President Minné nearly doubled its numbers in three years. In his budget request to the legislature in 1964, he asked for funding to double to provide a 15 percent pay increase for the entire faculty and to add forty-three new positions. Fifty-five additional faculty greeted the class of 1970 as enrollment crept to over three thousand students. Good times had clearly arrived in Winona. Additional faculty slots, very beneficial when enrollments swelled, caused fiscal problems when those enrollments fell, however. By 1970, even though enrollment numbers remained high, demographers prophesied doom and gloom, noting that the swollen birth rate of the baby boom generation would soon end. This prediction panicked some policymakers. In 1972 enrollment fell for the first time, although hardly precipitously. The question became whether good management and a wise legislature could provide a sound solution to the impending fiscal woes.

Unfortunately, the answer seemed to be no. President Robert DuFresne did much to stem the tide, as noted previously. By creating the External Studies Program, he not only met a societal need, but the program also generated significant enrollment, so that only in one or two years did Winona State actually decline in real number of full-time students (or full-time equivalents—FTE's, as administrators call them). He asked students to help him solve the attrition problem of students leaving school before graduation, although the actual retention rate (75 to 80 percent) was already pretty good for a school of Winona's size and mission.

He bent over backwards to keep the students mollified, which led to some faculty criticism. For example, when students protested having class on a Friday, late in May 1967, and marched on his home, he gave them the day off but asked that they use "ordinary channels" hereafter. Two years later in February, students protested the calendar at a very late date, noting after a referendum vote that they preferred a week-long spring break (to go to Ft. Lauderdale in large numbers) rather than the two traditional shorter breaks. Once again, President DuFresne gave in, making the calendar change effective immediately to the dismay of faculty. Students served as voting members of the Academic Affairs and Curriculum Committee (A2C2) and on the Faculty Tenure and Promotion Committee. President DuFresne supported a student demand that faculty pay fees to use Kryzsko Commons. Finally, when students demanded an end to the grade *F*, to be replaced with *NC* (no credit), he relented again, at least for freshmen and sophomores. (The faculty restored the *F* two years later.) In short, President DuFresne did much to appease students, for better or worse, possibly because he believed that news of further campus protests might adversely affect funding. In any event, he did preside over an era of relative tranquility, and WSU fared well, even acquiring the long-desired "university status" by 1975, the year before Dr. DuFresne resigned his presidency.

As enrollments reached three thousand, a new administrative structure was required. By 1968, in addition to a vice president of academic affairs, three deans came aboard, one for the College of Education, one for the College of Liberal Arts and Sciences, and one for the Graduate School.

Many believed the university's future lay in expanding its graduate programs. That year the legislature debated for the first time the possibility of the state colleges offering PhDs. The system also embraced a "Common Market Plan," the forerunner of the Minnesota Transfer Curriculum, which allowed juniors and seniors to transfer to any state university to complete their degree. But the most serious issue was funding. During the mid-1970s tuition began to increase; students now paid about one-third of their instructional cost. Senator Walter Mondale advocated legislation offering more loan money to students, and federal grants began to supplement local loans. In reality, however, even the increased tuition dollars did not allow the university sufficient flexibility to control its own destiny in times of financial hardship. Yet at the same time, students worked more and more hours to earn money to pay tuition: 65 percent of students worked by the early 1970s. Perhaps these economic pressures also helped to explain the grade inflation and cheating which crept into the culture of Winona State as well as all other institutions around the nation.

Given the limited resources, the reduced appropriation, and the funding formula as it then stood, President DuFresne announced he would have to cut at least three faculty positions, the first time this had occurred since 1876. Although relying on the seniority system, he asked the Faculty Senate to help him identify the victims. He informed the college community that the legislature provided funding for one faculty salary for every 19 students, and so mathematically the faculty of 218 (for an enrollment of 3,889) was 13 or 14 too many in theory. Students took the opportunity to protest tenure, asking why some of the poorer teachers remained while favorites like Dave Gross in English were let go. DuFresne also pointed out that, in his decision making, he did not want to damage growing programs like nursing and business. By the end of the year, four faculty were cut in the library, English, physics, foreign language and business education (the latter two half-time). In later years, the mandatory retirement age of sixty-eight would help reduce the pressure, although a number of well-qualified faculty, under pressure, retired earlier than they wished. The chancellor, a new position created in the 1960s to head the state college and then the state university system, suggested the elimination of "duplicative programs" to resolve the problem, but the difficulty in defining such programs made his idea impractical.

Building on the rudimentary structure already in place, the faculty moved quickly to form a union in response to the cuts. Back in the 1930s the faculty of the state's teachers' colleges had formed the Inter-Faculty Policy Committee, which offered recommendations to the Board and the legislature. During the 1960s, the organization was renamed the

Inter-Faculty Organization (IFO) and continued to represent the faculty on a statewide basis although the entity lacked teeth. Many faculty already belonged to a moderate organization, the American Association of University Professors (AAUP), which supported the notion of collective bargaining for university faculty. When the legislature passed the Public Employees Labor Relations Act (PELRA) in 1974, the faculty responded quickly by transforming the IFO into a bona fide union. Over the next year and a half, the faculty and the newly renamed State University Board (SUB) hammered out the Master Contract, which with some modifications, remains in existence today. Over the years, this agreement has established formal processes for matters such as tenure and promotion, and has protected faculty from arbitrary and capricious administrators like those who attempted to rule Winona State in the late 1970s and early 1980s.

Rising energy costs resulting from the energy crisis of the early 1970s placed more financial pressure on WSU. Although some suggested closing the campus during winter quarter, the school adopted less drastic measures. The athletic program reduced intramurals as temperatures in Memorial fell to fifty-eight degrees. Women complained about cold showers: the hot water temperature had been turned down to eighty-two degrees in order to comply with the governor's order to cut energy consumption by 25 percent. In the face of all this dismal news, President DuFresne decided that ten years in the presidency was enough and announced his resignation. Although he had faced many challenges, he had generally steered his ship of state well. Unfortunately, his successors would not have his good fortune and good sense. (DuFresne returned to teaching and made a bid to serve as state representative from the district but lost decisively in the election.)

Soon the field of presidential candidates narrowed, and the State University Board selected Robert Hanson, formerly the registrar and then the vice president for academic affairs at Moorhead State University. Another appointee with a degree in education, Hanson talked in his inaugural address about the need to create a development office (which he did in 1977) and the importance of creating a strategy to deal with the fiscal crisis. Unfortunately, he really had no vision. Although he talked in the abstract about the importance of liberal arts, stated the need to build the business faculty, and tossed a bone to students by advocating liquor on campus, from the very beginning of his administration he was inept. When the legislature announced no increase in funding for the next biennium, while an arbitrator awarded a 14 percent raise across the board, the administration faced a real crisis. The Board agreed to a small tuition hike, but that alone would not suffice. As the budget looked worse, lines hardened, bringing a systemwide faculty demand for the chancellor's resignation. At the local level, the administration planned to resolve budget problems in 1979 by retrenching (firing) four tenured faculty. The president compounded his woes and lost credibility offering publicly that the university could experience a $385,000 cut (about 20 percent of the budget appropriation) without doing any damage. To make matters worse, WSU's students voted against the idea of a tuition surcharge to balance the budget, although the Board dismissed the result.

Not surprisingly, a faculty survey taken in the spring of 1981 proved quite negative, with Hanson being rated as a fair to poor president because, in their opinion, he acted capriciously. Trust diminished to such a degree that faculty leaders tried to tape-record meet-and-confer sessions, at which idea Hanson became apoplectic, and stormed out of the room. Helen Popovich (who as dean of liberal arts had implemented a successful general education review that had increased the number of liberal arts credits by creating the "different culture" requirement, and reduced the number of PE credits required to graduate) was elevated to acting vice president for academic affairs. Hanson also created a dean of business and industry apart from education.

For a moment, hope existed. The Board allowed for consecutive 9 percent tuition hikes, and, despite predictions, enrollment went up to 4,650. But the dwindling appropriation from the state made balancing the budget impossible. The *Star Tribune* predicted that three state universities, Winona, Mankato, and Southwest, would be closed. By the spring of 1982, even with tuition increases of 15 percent for the fall, the chancellor projected a budget shortfall of over a million dollars for Winona State. This was real money! No solution other than cuts presented itself. The pressure on President Hanson must have been terrific, and no doubt contributed to the stroke he suffered at age fifty-four. Because the surgery for the brain aneurism went well, the Board decided to appoint the acting vice president, Helen Popovich, as acting president, expecting Dr. Hanson to recover and resume his presidency.

No greater disaster could have befallen WSU. She and her acting vice president, James Spear, responded to fiscal crisis by enacting draconian cuts while at the same time restructuring the faculty. No conversation accompanied the drama; the administration made no overtures to the faculty to think creatively about the university's problems. Dr. Popovich rejected cutting the bare minimum number of faculty in order to survive the crisis. Rather, she took the opportunity to cut deeper, allegedly taking out political enemies to build programs she favored. Rumors placed the number of faculty to be cut at fourteen, sixteen, and sometimes nineteen.

Eventually sixteen faculty, twelve of them tenured, received the news that they would receive a year's severance pay and then be terminated effective in the fall of 1983 while Popovich proposed hiring twelve new faculty in "growth" areas. History in particular was hard hit, with three faculty lost. Geography and photography ceased to exist as majors. After examining the budget carefully, the faculty proposed a different plan, suggesting measures that would have protected all tenured faculty. Popovich would have none of it.

Acting courageously, Faculty Association President Rod Henry and a busload of concerned faculty walked into the SUB meeting, dropped their alternative proposal on the table, and informed the Board that the faculty had taken a no-confidence vote on Popovich. In the end, the Board refused to read the faculty's thirteen-page report documenting complaints against the acting president (specifically for abusing her powers of retrenchment and being a poor communicator), but they did agree to launch a formal search for a new leader. Dr. Hanson officially resigned (he never regained his mental faculties and died in 2006), and Dr. Popovich announced that the "informal rule of tradition" would not allow her to become a candidate for the position. With a gloomy fiscal forecast again for 1984 and Governor Rudy Perpich talking about ending reciprocity and closing campuses, the university badly needed a breath of fresh air.

Although it had grown extraordinarily in all ways in the 1960s, WSU faced its most challenging times since the era of the great fire and the Depression during the decade from 1974 to 1983. While some positive developments occurred, such as the acquisition of university status, the school had stagnated. Many of the problems were not of its own making. The changing demographics affected funding, although too often local administrators, lacking in vision and intellectual curiosity, overreacted. The university did a good job of maintaining enrollment, vis-à-vis its competitors, even as the pool of traditional-aged college-bound students diminished. Aggressive marketing, new programs, and President Robert DuFresne's idea of providing education for nontraditional students all helped. But the smaller enrollments were also accompanied by declining tax revenues, as the 1970s recession continued for some time. No bold solutions emerged to deal with the crisis, and for the destructive presidents of the era, Robert Hanson and Helen Popovich, cutting faculty without consultation represented a misguided opportunity to transform the institution. Such grandiose schemes seldom work, and they failed in this instance as well. Worse yet, the adversarial relationship left a residue of ill-feeling and resentment that would last, in some instances, for decades. The new president would have a difficult task healing this gaping wound.

The Healing Begins under President Stark

After the bloodletting events of the spring of 1983, the campus needed a cleansing breath. The dismissal of tenured faculty and the cutting of programs had upset faculty and students alike, and campus morale sank. Fortunately, the arrival of a new president did much to reverse the downward trend. Dr. Thomas Stark, who had been a high school principal as well as an administrator at Mankato State University, had the personality and the skills to change the direction of the university. Knowing that the layoffs lay at the heart of the resentment, Stark made his first priority a review of the dismissals. Within a relatively short time, he rescinded all of the firings. With a collective sigh of relief, faculty returned to the classroom, and very slowly the icy relations and "smoldering resentment" between faculty and administration started to improve. The arrival of a new vice president, Dr. Chuck Sorensen, also contributed to more harmonious working relationships.

Not that the university did not face other challenges. Rochester, long a partner with Winona State, demanded more attention. City leaders there campaigned for an institution in their city that would grant four-year degrees, and Governor Perpich agreed. President Stark's solution was to propose a "2 + 2" for the Rochester campus—where students could take their basic classes at the community college and then transfer into select upper division programs that Winona State would provide in Rochester. For nursing, in particular, this provided an ideal situation, given Rochester's Mayo Clinic and interest in the health-care industry. Other programs included education, educational leadership, chemistry, business, psychology, and eventually social work. Although the Rochester community did not entirely embrace this solution, the WSU offerings at Rochester have served thousands of students over the years. While the city's demographics would change in the 1990s and the programming would be modified, the partnership continues to the present day.

Despite the uncertainties in Rochester, WSU seemed more optimistic about its future. Even though enrollments had stagnated at around forty-five hundred students, at least they did not precipitously decline, as the gloomy state demographer had predicted. More importantly, students and faculty seemed happier. The faculty settled their contract. Student satisfaction reached an all-time high. Sensitive to the tensions of the previous years, students now reported a much more positive atmosphere on campus. An evaluation ranked WSU's academics the highest in the system and ahead of even excellent private schools like Carleton and St. Olaf—a conclusion that may have made its findings suspect! Students felt well treated by Student Affairs personnel and generally were pleased with their experience. In short, an era of good feelings had begun to take hold at Winona State, although it would take many years before faculty would forgive and forget the negative actions of the late 1970s and early 1980s.

The University Comes of Age

Chapter 4

Like the Mississippi River flowing near the campus, Winona State University has changed its direction over the years, swept by raging storms over policy and droughts of finances. As previous chapters have related, the university weathered these challenges: the great fire, the Depression, the world wars, and the turmoil of the 1970s and early 1980s. What should be the mission of the school, conceived as a teacher-training institution but now so much more? How did the university relate to the community, now that it had significantly outgrown its original physical footprint on Wapasha's Prairie? Would the institution be able to keep pace with burgeoning technology, unleashed initially by Sputnik and the space race? These questions and more faced administration, faculty, staff, and students as the wounds described in chapter 3 began to heal.

The march to WSU's sesquicentennial has turned out to be a tale of progress with a few difficult moments. The adverse circumstances of the 1970s and 1980s helped the university regain its vision and sense of purpose. With superior leadership after 1984, Winona State reasserted itself as one of the finest institutions in the upper Midwest, able to offer both undergraduate and graduate students high-quality educations. Even though the presidency has changed hands three times during the last twenty-three years, each chief executive in his or her own way provided the leadership that served the college well, a significant improvement from the years just before. Facing challenges together, faculty, staff, students, alumni, and community members helped build the great institution that occupies the campus today. The university has regained its vision to serve as an instrument for the public good while raising standards and promoting quality. Once again, the university has become an innovator in the field of public higher education.

Campus Regains Its Direction

The tumultuous years of the 1970s and 1980s left Winona State wandering purposelessly in a new age. Like many similar teacher education institutions, WSU had been promoted to the status of college and then university with little thought to its mission. Rather, sheer demand for higher education by the baby boomers had made the evolution of the institution a matter of expediency. During the 1990s however, the university became comfortable with its newly stated mission, "a community of learners improving our world." All constituencies favored a renewed commitment to academic excellence, more consistent with Winona's expectations in the late nineteenth century than in recent decades. In addition, the practical bent of the institution, which traditionally had served the societal needs of the upper Midwest, reaffirmed itself, but in new and broader ways.

For example, elevated admissions standards and the introduction of more academic rigor into the curriculum significantly improved the quality of the education offered. Beginning in the 1990s, the campus embraced the new systemwide initiative called Q-7, a grant-funded program promoting access with quality. Already in 1989 Winona State had created the nation's first degree program in composite engineering, a unique curriculum that matched the specialized needs of local industry. New faculty came to teach the classes, and a new building, Stark Hall, was constructed in part to house the program and its necessary equipment. The composite engineering program secured accreditation, already held by its joint tenant in Stark, the nursing program. Because of the growth of high-quality regional medical facilities like the Mayo Clinic and Gundersen-Lutheran Hospital, demand for trained nurses spiraled. As a result, not only did the university initiate a highly successful master's program in nursing, but by the time of the sesquicentennial, it had unveiled an applied doctor of nursing practice (DNP) initiative for health-care providers. Other programs as well achieved national accreditation: teachers' education, paralegal, social work, music, theatre, and corrections to name a few. For the more traditional liberal arts and sciences students, the new Residential College offered opportunities to engage in thematic and interdisciplinary courses coupled with more rigorous reading, writing, and analytical experiences. Individual students and faculty received praise for their work. A nursing student, Betsy Motschenbacher, became the president of the National Student Nurses Association in 1985, and a decade later, a paralegal, Terese Kiefer Wilkie, won one of two scholarships funded by the National Paralegal Association. The system faculty named Dr. Susan Hatfield the outstanding teacher in the state university system in 1993, and Dr. Richard Jarvinen received an award from NASA for explaining the theoretical reasons for the O-ring failure that caused the *Challenger* disaster. Unfortunately, time and space prevent naming all the programs and individuals whose collective and individual accomplishments have contributed to the university's march towards excellence.

With the appointment of Dr. Darrell Krueger as president in 1989, Winona State returned to its nineteenth-century tradition of picking chief executives who had made a professional reputation nationally; this, not surprisingly led to even greater achievements on campus. Perhaps the most important reason the State University Board selected Krueger was because of his national reputation in the area of assessment. A deeply ethical and principled leader, Dr. Krueger's seventeen-year presidency left a major imprint on WSU. In any event, assessment of programs and the university as a whole began in the early 1990s, boosted later in the decade with the receipt of a major federal grant to implement data-driven assessment on campus. With politicians and the population at large clamoring for greater accountability in the world of higher education, assessment seemed the best way to demonstrate that WSU students, and society as a whole, received benefits from their time at the university. Assessment also allowed programs and the university itself to demonstrate continuous improvement. Tweaking little flaws in the system led to greater student satisfaction and improved classroom performances.

With the arrival on campus in 2005 of our current president, Dr. Judith Ramaley, who had two prior presidencies and a stint as an education leader at the National Science Foundation on her resumé, the quest for quality took another step forward with the L-21 (Learning for the Twenty-First Century) initiative. Grounded in the belief that innovation and change must occur as the result of a scholarly act, L-21 offers students unique opportunities. For example, the new major in global studies, expanded study-abroad programs, and international travel opportunities mean that many WSU students will spend time overseas during the course of their studies. For others an internship experience in a diverse community (such as ongoing efforts to help rebuild hurricane-ravaged New Orleans), will broaden horizons and expand cultural awareness. Students will hone their research skills by undertaking discipline-specific investigations, much like those they will encounter in their professional careers.

Meanwhile, the university continues to focus on its strong basic programs like education and the liberal arts and sciences. To prepare students better for tomorrow's challenges, in 2000 the faculty revamped the general education program, now called University Studies, a great change from the "commons" of the 1930s. Perhaps the most innovative university studies reform responded to a wider societal concern that too many graduates lacked the basic skills that to employers seemed fundamental. As a result, the faculty created a system of flagged courses that re-emphasized writing, oral communication, and critical thinking within majors. Many departments adopted a capstone experience for their students, providing the opportunity to conduct research and work with faculty members in small groups.

Policy changes also enhanced academics. For at least a generation, Winona State had gained a reputation as a "suitcase campus," where the majority of students took three-day weekends and went home throughout the academic year. (Most classes met Monday through Thursday, although many science labs were scheduled on Fridays.) In the early 1990s, the faculty agreed to the current Monday/Wednesday/Friday or Tuesday/Thursday schedule for classes. In the winter of 1995, the state legislature mandated a transition from quarters to semesters, putting WSU again in step with the vast majority of institutions across the nation. These calendar changes kept students on campus longer, enhancing learning, allowing for more in-depth experiences, and facilitating research and writing in upper-division classes. But no change brought more dramatic consequences then elevating admissions standards. From the era of virtual open admissions in the early 1980s, standards improved until at the very least students needed a competitive ACT of 21 or a class ranking in the top half to matriculate. No wonder faculty felt they could challenge their students with a more rigorous curriculum! And students responded positively. Retention rates increased significantly after 2000, presumably because Winona became a more desirable institution.

To make an institution truly academic, the college library must become the focal point (or at least one of the focal points) of campus. For many years students complained about the inadequacies of Maxwell Library. More a lounge for socializing, the library lacked both adequate materials and sufficient staff. Two alternatives emerged in the 1980s: to add on to the architectural hodgepodge known as Maxwell, or to build an entirely new structure on the site of the tennis courts. For years, the campus priority remained revamping the football stadium, until the new president, Darrell Krueger, and the Faculty Senate agreed to promote the library first. Because several universities wanted to upgrade their libraries, the system created a task force to design the "library of the future." Soon, with the leadership of Gene Pelowski, an alum and state legislator, planning money followed, and after some probably needless bureaucratic delays, actual construction began in the late 1990s. In the fall of 1999, Governor Jesse Ventura arrived on campus for the public dedication of what is now known as the Darrell Krueger Library. The modern facility saw cataloging switch to the Library of Congress system, all on-line, and the addition of many technological databases to assist faculty and student research. Besides being wonderful advocates for the new building during the legislative bonding hearings, students also contributed by offering a tuition surcharge to pay for new acquisitions. By the turn of the century, the campus again had a library, as it had in the nineteenth century, suitable to serving the academic mission of the institution. Student usage significantly increased, to the point that WSU won national recognition for library activity, especially after students demanded and received extended library hours as they did when the original Maxwell Library was built in the 1930s.

Discussion about the new library meant a more vital intellectual community, the benefits of which affected other parts of campus as well. The Theater and Music Departments expanded their offerings, and the annual Dancescape and Madrigal Dinner grew in popularity to the point that tickets became hard to obtain. A new Mayo-sponsored lecture series brought large crowds to hear about science and society. The English Department received a grant to create the Great River Reading Series, which brought novelists, essayists, and poets to campus; not only did local writers receive invitations, but people from all over the country came to read their creative works. Dean Troy Paino and political science professor Matt Bosworth created a forum whereby Liberal Arts and Science faculty could present their research to peers, and English professor Jim Armstrong initiated meaningful scholarly exchanges such as the annual Celebration of the Book. The library's Athenaeum series organized by Joe Mount and Kendall Larson opened a similar venue to students, faculty, and staff. With the collaboration of the Theatre du Mississippi, the Frozen River Film Festival gave the academic community something with which to amuse and stimulate itself during the dreary cold days of February. Most importantly for the community, the arrival of the Great River Shakespeare Festival in 2004 brought an academic and cultural environment to campus year round.

Of course, throughout the 1980s and 1990s interesting speakers had continued to come to campus. For example, G. Gordon Liddy, self-styled defender of democracy (and convicted Watergate burglar) regaled audiences in the early 1980s. Many students heard Senator Bob Dole speak at nearby St. Mary's in 1987. When Darrell Krueger came to the university in 1989, he persuaded the WSU Foundation to fund the Lyceum series, which provided monies to bring notables to campus. Over the next decade, Elie Weisel talked to enthralled audiences about the horrors of the Holocaust and the importance of remembering those lost. Stephen Covey expounded his very successful theories of management and self-improvement, and Maya Angelou recited her poetry and left the stage with a message of hope and harmony. Kurt Vonnegut read from his fiction, and former Senator Eugene McCarthy returned to campus to discuss 1968. Less well-known speakers included a former Hezbollah captive in Lebanon (who had been tortured); feminist educational theorist Jill Tarule, who celebrated the initiation of the Women's Studies program with an address; Mike Farrell (B. J. Hunnicut of TV's *M.A.S.H.*), who talked about international human rights cases; an advocate of the American Disabilities Act, who explained that complex piece of legislation to the campus; a former Red Guard from communist China who discussed the 1980s in that country; and various appearances of the wildly popular/wildly unpopular governor, Jesse Ventura, who engaged Chris Matthews of *Hardball* in political banter.

Individual faculty, as always, contributed to the intellectual livelihood of the campus by publishing and creating. (In a short history like this, one cannot name all those who produced works, and a partial list is bound to offend; consequently, a generic approach, while unsatisfactory, may serve best.) A number of the faculty in the English Department published novels and volumes of poetry, winning awards such as the Minnesota Book Award and the Iowa Short Fiction Award. One faculty member had her novel transformed into a television movie starring the orchidaceous Victoria Principal. A music faculty member's original symphony was performed by the La Crosse Symphony orchestra and a mass communications professor wrote several well-received textbooks (one of which drew the ire of Rush Limbaugh). Faculty in sociology, social work, and history, to name just a few, wrote monographs that advanced the state of knowledge in their particular disciplines. To a greater degree than ever before, faculty committed themselves to scholarly and creative acts, setting a fine example for students.

As Chancellor Robert Caruthers noted in his remarks about the Q-7 initiative, quality costs money, and over the twenty-three years under consideration here, ugly, pragmatic funding issues all too frequently outweighed academic concerns. Even in the days of milk and honey in the late 1990s, higher education consistently heard the clamor of politicians and bureaucrats yelling "cut, cut, Cut!" As with other public institutions across the country, students shouldered a disproportionate share of the financial burden, to the point where eventually tuition exceeded state funding in terms of percentage of the university budget. President Krueger chaired a statewide committee that attempted to create a new funding formula with an established, firm base that would have guaranteed quality, but the legislature never funded it. So students paid. To maintain quality and pay for concrete services (technology, library materials, access to classes) students agreed to tax themselves with a tuition surcharge. Thoughtful student presidents, including Adrienne Mitchell, Mike Swenson, and Jason Fossum, understood the need to improve the institution and their obligation as student leaders to consider the future and the legacy they would leave the next group of their colleagues. With their unified effort, the institution advanced and received recognition not only as one of the hundred "best buys" in the United States (and the only one in Minnesota) but also climbed in the *U.S. News and World Report* rankings, qualifying as a top-tier school in 2004. Unfortunately, as the quality of student leadership declined beginning in the fall of 2002, some of the momentum was lost.

In short, the twenty-three most recent years of Winona State's history have seen a resumption of the university's status as one of the academic leaders in the upper Midwest. While many traditions continued, such as high-quality programs, individual scholarly contributions, and distinguished on-campus events for the entire community, WSU in this era began to excel in new ways. Under improved presidential leadership, the university focused on a new mission consistent with its status as a university. Assessment brought a sense of accountability and left WSU in a position to prove its education made a difference. With a new library and programs that created a more academic focus, the university continued to advance. As the sesquicentennial approached, Winona State also began to think more about its relationship with the community outside the confines of campus, and it is to that subject that we now turn.

Community Relations: From Irritant to Emollient

Over the past twenty-five years, two major issues have driven apart the town-gown relationship. First, student relations with the community had become hostile because of alcohol-related behavior. Second, a fair percentage of students actually lived in the community, and the quantity and quality of their housing periodically led to landlord-tenant controversies. These two issues dominated the relationship between the city and the campus roughly until the turn of the century when a new focus emerged, and the campus began to respond to the call to make the community better. With the rise of volunteerism, relations improved. Service to community, academically called "service learning," has taken root, becoming an important element of WSU's mission. Thus, the ideal of students fostering a cooperative relationship with the community, a longstanding but dormant tradition, came to the fore once again.

In 1985, the legislature raised the drinking age to twenty-one, and overnight created a new source of irritation between campus and community. After World War II, in particular, students' alcohol consumption increased, and in the permissive era of the 1960s and 1970s, with drinking legal at eighteen, a night frolicking in local taverns became standard fare.

Although drinking on campus could only occur legally on limited occasions, the rule was often winked-at by all concerned. Nevertheless, the 1985 statute, controversial as it was, made good sense for teens often did not handle alcohol responsibly. What had once been good sport for most students now became illegal for all but a minority. With bars turning away minors—though of course not all did, so raids resulted in arrests periodically—students turned to house parties as an alternative way of consuming alcohol. One or two students would buy a keg or two of beer legally, and then charge a dollar or two for all comers, turning a nice profit. (One house of roommates bragged they had paid for their entire educations this way.) Even back in the 1980s, police broke up house parties, arresting the juvenile drinkers they could catch. House parties in the late 1990s heightened concerns because of the dangers associated with binge drinking, although fortunately Winona did not experience the tragedies that occurred on several college campuses nationwide. Improved police enforcement, including foot patrols on nearby streets on Thursdays and weekends also seemed to create an impact, as neighbors asked the police for a greater presence.

No event brought the alcohol issue more to the forefront than Springfest, an off-campus and only semi-officially sponsored activity. Theoretically, Springfest was a great idea. After a cold, dark winter, what better way to celebrate the arrival of warm weather than an all-day Saturday party where students could catch some rays, listen to a good band or two, and have a good time? Unfortunately, the presence of unlimited alcohol transformed the event to a more negative objective: to get blasted. Broken bottles and trash littered Lake Park and neighborhood yards, and more than one residence had its shrubbery watered in an undesirable way. Early in the 1990s the administration voiced the idea that Springfest "needed to be brought within the mission of the University," but reform attempts came to nought. Finally, after a decade of existence, Springfest came to a halt in 1997. The new semester calendar played a role as well. Instead of late May commencements, graduation now occurred nearly a month earlier, and April weather could be a bit dicey for an outdoor party with expensive bands. As a compromise, block parties by the residence halls replaced Springfest, bringing cleaner fun to campus and cooling off a tense issue between town and gown.

Given that WSU continued to be largely residential, with those students not housed in residence halls mostly living in apartments in older homes near the university, the question of the quality and quantity of housing also brought tension between college and community. Students complained about drafty houses in winter, landlords who refused to make repairs, and the seedy circumstances in which some were forced to live. For a variety of reasons, some of them imposed by Minnesota's regulatory system and some out of simple greed since demand for housing outstripped supply, landlords did little to improve their properties. Tenants' cars littered yards and blocked driveways, again irking neighbors who demanded the university build a prohibitively expensive ramped garage for the excess vehicles. As the university opened new housing at the East Lake apartments and the Tau Center, the law of supply and demand swung against the landlords, who now found their apartments vacant. As a result, many upgraded their buildings and provided more amenities, like the Internet service already available in university housing. Further, the campus found additional parking near the new residence halls, and purchased the Lincoln School, just beyond the current circumference of the campus, as a potential place for additional parking.

Although underage drinking and housing remained irritants, they became less important in the new century. Like many universities across the country, Winona State found itself becoming more involved with its city in a positive, uplifting way. Maybe the passing of "Generation X" in the late 1990s made the big difference; maybe a new idealism struck a spark. In any event WSU made more concrete efforts to implement that part of its mission statement that referred to the university being dedicated to "improving the world." Certainly, some attempts at better community relations had occurred in the early 1980s. The postsecondary education option (PSEO) offered bright high school students in the region the chance to earn college credits. But many attempts to integrate students and the city, like the Fall Fling of 1985 and the Great Winona Get-Together four years later fizzled. A decade later, the climate had changed. Coach Tom Sawyer harangued the football team about their need to become involved in the community. Students, faculty, and staff pitched in to sandbag the streets of Fountain City during the spring flood of 2001. A large number of students volunteered as Big Brothers and Big Sisters. Colette Hyman, a WSU faculty member, was named "Volunteer of the Year" in 2001 by the city, and after the tragedies of 9-11 and Hurricane Katrina, many offered to help. Service learning became a critical element of the L-21 discussion, not only as practical training, but also to reinforce the values necessary for an engaged democratic society as taught in university studies courses. As the sesquicentennial approached, the "Adopt-a-block" program, where student volunteers helped clean up neighborhoods on a weekend in the spring, evoked a tremendous response. In short, relations between the university and community changed for the better in the twenty-first century.

Student Activities: Old and New Traditions

Despite what the faculty hoped, not every student spent all their time at his or her books. In addition to community involvement, many students engaged in other extracurricular activities. Even more than previous generations, students had to work to pay for their education. Attempts by administrators to limit the number of hours of employment failed, but the university did try to find students more academically related work on campus. By the time of this printing, over 110 clubs and extracurricular organizations exist on campus, and over 20 percent of students participate in one or more of them. With a variety of interests represented, from the oldest club on campus, the Wenonah Players, to the new Hispanic Club and the originally controversial GLAD organization (the gay and lesbian club), groups existed to meet a variety of student interests. The nature of religious clubs changed during these decades. Less denominationally focused, Christian organizations reached out to a broader spectrum of students, while the Muslim Student Association demonstrated a growing campus interest in religious diversity. Although traditional religion remained important to WSU students, fraternities and sororities had their ups and downs. In 1987, the last frat, Sigma Tau Gamma, closed its doors because of a lack of membership, but a few years later, Tau Kappa Epsilon and others revived their charters, and now the campus again has a vibrant Greek life.

Athletics attracted many students, and particularly during the Krueger era the university enjoyed some competitive successes. Surviving the furor over the dismissal of a winning but unpopular football coach, the Warriors under Tom Sawyer won a number of conference championships and the Mineral Water Bowl in 2000. Longtime baseball coach Gary Grob recorded over a thousand victories and in the process brought several league championships to Winona. Women's sports did well in the 1980s: the gymnastics team finished as high as third nationally, and one of its outstanding members, Katie Dempsey, won All-American honors. As the university provided more funding for women's intercollegiate athletes, as a result of Title IX, the women's soccer team responded by reeling off a series of championships. The minor sports, too, recorded occasional success, like the women's golf team and the Warriorettes, who received national recognition for their dance routines in 1993. With the arrival of a new athletic director, Larry Holstad, in 1997, who insisted on academics first with his athletes, sports became better integrated into campus life. Of course, not all was perfect: athlete assaults on fellow students and altercations with the police raised issues of special treatment.

Overall, however, athletes achieved great successes without succumbing to swelled heads. Without a doubt the most notable achievement was that of the men's basketball team, which won the NCAA Division II title in the spring of 2006 against the defending national champion, Virginia Union, Winona State's first-ever national championship. Fans, including President Judith Ramaley, flew to Springfield, Massachusetts, to cheer at the final game, and alumni and friends all over the country watched the televised broadcast.

Still, not every student played sports or joined clubs. For many, the traditional calendar-related events provided an opportunity to participate in extracurricular activities. Above all others, Homecoming retained its popularity, although its format continued to change. For a time, Second City, a Chicago-based comedy group, became an institution at the event, as did the parade with local bands, the pep rally, the football game, and the crowning of the king and queen. By the mid-1990s, however, attendance had become so thin at the dance (allegedly only the royalty and their court ever showed up) that other activities were substituted. By now the old Spring Prom had given way to other events in particular, the Mr. WSU and later the Miss WSU contest. The former, more a burlesque comedy show than anything else, featured cross-dressing and raucous humor. Campus critics urged that the Miss WSU contest be more than a beauty contest, and that the woman selected represent school spirit and community values. In fact, funds raised at these events were donated to medical research. Parents' weekend, sometimes a spring event, gave students a chance to show off their surroundings to those who made their attendance possible. Slowly, alcohol became less a feature at official school events. In the 1970s, Student Affairs staff had created the orientation tradition of "beerball" (softball plus beer) at the lake; by the late 1980s that had ended. So, too, did the informal traditions of heavy drinking by those participating in the Homecoming Parade.

During the year, Student Affairs arranged for a variety of types of popular entertainment, often musical or comedic. Early in their careers, comedians like Jay Leno and Adam Sandler tested their routines on WSU audiences. (Garrison Keillor and Chris Matthews broadcast their shows from Somsen and the Performing Arts Center.) Big name musical acts included Joan Jett and John Cafferty, Cheap Trick, two-time Grammy winner Nelly, and Bowling for Soup. These spring concerts, however, cost great sums: sometimes the bands played too little, and at other times, the concerts did not adequately draw. Costs and student apathy made Student Affairs' job much more difficult. Yet a good concert remained a big draw, and the tradition continued, as did other student activities.

The men's basketball team won the NCAA Division II national championship in 2006 and finished second in 2007. Along the way they set a new Division II win-streak record, winning fifty-seven games in a row before losing on a last second shot in the national championship.

MassMutual
FINANCIAL GROUP

Sex remained popular. Although twenty-four-hour visitation in the dorms had become institutionalized, related issues required solutions. A soft-hearted Student Affairs staffer, lionized by some for never saying "no" to students, approved putting condom machines in the student union. Once word filtered into the community, however, some alumni and Foundation Board members questioned the morality of the decision. When President Krueger arrived on campus, he nixed the idea, only to face a resurrected proposal several years later. After a useful debate focusing on health concerns, the administration allowed machines on a limited basis in the residence halls. Infrequently, sexual crimes occurred on campus. These ranged in seriousness from occasional stalkers, men peeking under shower curtains, or flashers hiding around campus (one caught by Professor Tim Hatfield, who jogged alongside and persuaded the culprit to turn himself in) to full-fledged sexual assaults, both date rape and stranger rape. Periodically, debates about the morality of casual sex and abortion took place on campus, mirroring similar discussions around the country. Students came up with ways to protect themselves from violent crime, initiating the idea of the Code Blue emergency phones around campus, suggesting the installation of security cameras in many locations, and raising consciousness by participating in "Take Back the Night" marches. Even at its worst moments, the campus ranked as one of the safest in the country, a comfort especially to parents.

Nevertheless, on occasion WSU students (and, yes, faculty and staff) found themselves in difficulty with the law. Throughout the period, enforcement of drug laws brought the most students to the hoosegow, some for more serious offenses than others. Very occasionally, students pulled knives on each other and made bomb threats to get out of exams; once a student aimed a shotgun at a colleague. Among other felons were a forged-check schemer and a counterfeiter. (WSU's most notorious criminal, the woman convicted of strangling her baby, took correspondence courses from the University of Minnesota while serving her sentence and transferred to the Minneapolis campus upon her release.) Generally, however, the vast majority of WSU students led honest lives.

Some students became involved in political issues, both on and beyond the campus. Students successfully spoke out against a proposed rule that would have limited protests to specific times and places. (Such free speech zones on other campuses have been ruled constitutional by the US Supreme Court.) And, indeed, student protests and suggestions have led to a number of improvements over the years. In addition to the aforementioned Code Blue safety lights, students also convinced the administration to change food services to the much more palatable

Chartwells, to ban smoking in campus buildings, to create an Answer Center in Kryzko Commons, and to convert vacated space in Maxwell Library to an exercise facility, the Wellness Center. Because enrollments had increased dramatically during the early twenty-first century, intramural programs could no longer meet student needs. Likewise, the varsity teams lacked proper training facilities. Thus, the Wellness Center in Maxwell met a significant need until a larger and more comprehensive building could be constructed. In 1995, students wisely voted not to change the university's name and become a cookie-cutter copy of other institutions in the system (Minnesota State University at Winona) or worse yet, a pale imitation of the popular TV show *Coach*. When the size of the graduating class swelled to the point of limiting tickets for family members, students helped draft the proposal for a split commencement, as well as a separate commencement at the end of fall semester.

Students, along with a concerned administration and faculty, also helped the WSU community open its eyes to issues of race and discrimination. Given the campus's location and the traditional student population, the university struggled with diversity issues. Vice President Cal Winbush labored long to promote cultural diversity, advocating ways to increase the number of African-Americans on campus, though his efforts succeeded only modestly. More successfully, concerned campus community members helped heighten awareness. Black Cultural Awareness Week morphed into a full month of Black History events highlighted by the very popular Soul Food Dinner in the 1990s. The administration committed itself to increasing the number of minority scholarships, and as a result, minority enrollment increased. Special recruiters also brought new students to the campus. Soon the university had a full-fledged cultural diversity plan, designed not only to improve numbers but also retention and graduation rates. When the national furor arose over celebrating Martin Luther King Day in 1989, some WSU students participated in the protest mounted in Rochester. Open forums on campus stimulated further discussions about race. No more dramatic incident occurred than in the aftermath of the arrest and roughing up of two black football players by the Winona police in 1994 for allegedly disturbing the peace. When the subsequent investigation showed the police had overreacted, the city mandated cultural sensitivity training for the force. Students' response was sympathetic, and the clearly innocent party in the incident, Rudy Story, was voted the next year's homecoming king.

Other minority groups also expanded their presence. By far the largest group on campus was the international students, with numbers approaching four hundred (5 percent of the student body). Proudly displaying their

International students make up by far the largest minority group on campus (5 percent of the student body). Here the students proudly display their national flags at President Judith Ramaley's inauguration in 2005. The annual International Student Dinner has been a campus tradition for many years.

respective nations' flags on occasions such as the annual International Student Dinner, these students broadened majority perspective by interacting in classes, sharing tables in the dining halls, and participating in clubs and in President Ramaley's inauguration. Majority students also signed up for study abroad programs, not just to Scandinavia and England any more, but to places as remote as Mongolia. By the late 1990s, Mexico had become the spring break destination of choice (not that Corona and Club Boom constituted a real cultural experience). The Hispanic Club represented another fast-growing minority, although the new calendar with its early end to spring semester caused contortions for the Cinco de Mayo festival. Following a well-publicized gay-bashing incident off-campus, gay, lesbian and bisexual students determined to express themselves, and sponsored a Gay Pride festivity. Likewise, a Disability Awareness Fair made more students aware of the problems facing those with physical handicaps. Despite the progress made during recent decades, all agree that further work should be accomplished in this arena.

In short, student activities largely remained what they had always been, a recreational opportunity, yet still part of the experience of reaching full maturity. Some activities were sponsored and met with the full approval of the university community, while others were not. Many served as experiences that furthered the idea of the university, particularly team sports where athletes fought for the common good. These moments, especially the capture of a national basketball championship, helped to boost school spirit and raise the purple-and-white banners high. Other school-sponsored activities also furthered the mission, especially service opportunities that helped others. Theater and music helped make students more professional in their disciplines, and the championship forensic teams of the 1980s helped foster students' ability to debate important public issues. Whatever the outcome, properly organized student activities remained an important part of the student learning experience and over the decades reflected changing values. From the "Generation X" of the 1980s to the more public-spirited students of today, traditions remained powerful but modified to keep pace with the changing times.

Rebuilding the Financial Base

During this period, Winona State made the transition from a state-supported institution to a state-assisted one. Even when the state prospered and revenues climbed, other agencies claimed the new tax money. K–12 education, health care, and correctional institutions grabbed policymakers' attention, while higher education became a lower priority. Some analysts blamed the changed mission of the institution. While once preparing graduates to serve the public good directly as teachers, now these institutions took on primarily a private purpose, or at least a less well-defined public purpose, though arguably today's more lucrative careers in law, medicine, engineering, and business do serve the public, in different ways. As the percentage of the budget provided by the state's allocation diminished, administrators had to develop new ways to make up the shortfall. Unlike some other states, where external fundraising efforts supplemented a steady and certain state subsidy, at Winona State any the new monies had to help balance the budget.

For the first time in the institution's history, private donations became important. In days of yore, pursuing such funding seemed irrelevant for two reasons. First, the State of Minnesota provided adequate monies, at least for the most part, to keep WSU operating. Second, when all or nearly all graduates taught school, the alumni did not earn enough to make pursuing them with pledge cards worthwhile. By the 1980s, however, the situation had changed, and like many institutions, Winona State decided to make its Foundation an important revenue-securing entity. Created in 1963 to serve as the legal beneficiary of two generous bequests, the Winona State Foundation grew slowly at first. The first big cash gift, over $300,000 came in 1984, allegedly to create an endowed chair in mathematics. (The money seems to have gone for some other purpose eventually.) Two years later IBM donated an in-kind gift of both hardware and software valued at $750,000. The following year President Thomas Stark, a great conciliator but not the most forward-thinking administrator, decided to abolish the position of vice president of development, and downgraded fundraising to a lesser role. By the mid-1990s under President Darrell Krueger, vice presidents Gary Evans and later Jim Schmidt expanded the development function, reaching out to alumni, faculty, local businessmen, and friends of the institution like Ben Miller and Lewis Younger among others. An annual fund drive raised substantial amounts from faculty and staff. Given its late start in the fundraising game, the development office made significant strides forward, although WSU's very nature as a public institution made alumni less interested in giving than those at private institutions, where giving back was an established part of the culture.

Despite the growth of the development office and its successes, these funds provided only a partial solution. Grants, too, proved disappointing for a number of reasons. First, the quantity of grant money coming into the university, at least through 2007, remained relatively small. Secondly, grant money came for a specific purpose, and once the "soft money" disappeared, the institution had to discover new ways to pay for keeping these positions and services. Nevertheless, grants, among them the $700,000 for the nursing program in 1997 and the 1999 $1.3 million Department of Education assessment grant, helped the institution enormously. In each instance, the grant money challenged Winona to move forward in a new and positive direction, which, even after the external funding ended, was deemed worthy enough to continue. Federal money also led to the establishment of the National Child Protection Training Center, another example of Winona State's commitment to furthering the public good. Compared to outright gifts, however, grants proportionately made up a very small portion of the budget.

Looking back over newspapers from 1990 on, one is amazed to see the words *budget crisis* and *budget cuts* reiterated year after year. How discouraging this cry must have been to a visionary president, and how taxing on the imaginations of everybody at the university. Even the pro-education governor Rudy Perpich at one time talked about closing campuses (recall that Winona's name was among those circulated in 1984), and his successors in the 1990s also slashed and burned. Brief enrollment declines in the mid-1980s and mid-1990s triggered reductions under the then existing funding formula. Eventually the state forgot even its statutory obligations, simply funding institutions at a lower figure per pupil. Minnesota did not seem to be retaining its image as the "brain-state," a place where higher education mattered. Some policymakers blamed our competing university systems; others the lack of a centralized and efficient administration; others the existence of too many institutions for the population. An unwritten and probably outdated rule stated no student should be more than forty miles away from some higher education provider. By 1991, a key legislator decided that three of the systems—the state universities, the community colleges, and the technical institutes—needed to be merged into a single entity, now called Minnesota State Colleges and Universities (MnSCU). Once implemented, the new system proved to be the bloated, centralizing, and rule-driven bureaucracy that the faculty and many legislators feared, but at least from the legislature's viewpoint, having a single system with which to deal made more sense.

In terms of providing more funding, this new system did not help much. As a result, dictates came down to cut—as much as $1.2 million one year—and to stockpile a sizeable reserve. So the university looked at cutting specific athletic programs or eliminating noncontractual reassigned time for faculty. Belt-tightening governor Arne Carlson suggested a pay freeze for all public employees, a statement that moved Democratic-leaning faculty even further to the left. But none of these were long-term solutions. By 1992 the state tacitly made the decision to allow higher education institutions to balance the books on the backs of students. Fees for technology, parking, and a host of other services came into existence. Tuition rose 30 percent between 1991 and 1994, which angered some student leaders. Higher tuition, coupled with larger class sizes and no library acquisitions, hardly seemed to fulfill the promise of greater quality. But because of budget circumstances, tuition and fees had to increase at a more rapid rate. Even the fact that Winona's business office won system awards for efficiency and farsightedness could not help resolve the fiscal dilemma.

Approaching the problem imaginatively, the administration and student leaders decided that the only way these increases could be made palatable was if portions of the new revenues were dedicated to specific services that students wanted. As a result, a 1 percent surcharge helped to pay for improved technology one year, and another year a surcharge raised money for library materials and duplicating costs. But in the main, tuition increases simply offset revenue shortfalls, incurred even when WSU was more popular than ever. Enrollment skyrocketed as the sesquicentennial approached, with around eight thousand students now utilizing both campuses. By 2004, students had become fed up. Some of the frustration was understandable, as double-digit tuition increases became the norm at WSU just as they had across the nation. At the same time, many of the post-2002 student leaders suffered from myopia and became victims of self-interest. Consequently, for the first time in many years, fractious divisions emerged on campus with students balking at the costs of an initiative (the new university program discussed in the final section) that would have benefited future generations.

Technology at the Core of Campus

Over this last period, from 1984 to the present, technology changed student life and academics. While at the beginning of this era a professor who used colored chalk was on the cusp of the technology curve, by 2005 blackboards had given way to whiteboards—and they to PowerPoint and D2L (Desire to Learn) software. Beginning with IBM's gift of software and hardware in 1986, changes on campus occurred in rapid succession. Soon residence halls offered cable TV, and a video store opened in Kryzsko Commons. Student IDs now came equipped with barcodes, and over time the same IDs became cards that allowed students to charge goods and services. Other technological services, like the Internet, intended originally to be used for instructional purposes, also became instruments for e-mail, text-messaging, downloading favorite tunes, and allegedly (though the

Despite concerns with state appropriation cuts and tuition increases in the 1990s and into the twenty-first century, enrollment continued to increase. By 2007 it had reached eight thousand students.

author never saw any examples) for cheating on exams. For the contemporary student, technology had become a necessity, even while some faculty struggled with the change.

In addition to enriching student lives, technology also improved the mechanics of university operations, at least once the glitches were resolved. While some of us loved the old IBM "class card system," students had to stand in long registration lines to collect the cards they needed to enroll in their classes. After a failed attempt to create a telephone registration system, the university settled for an on-line system. Initially the students gave their preferred schedule to a keypunch operator, receiving a print-out of their classes at the end of the process. Finally, a MnSCU-led initiative created a homegrown web registration system. While the system sometimes crashed at most inconvenient moments, on the whole it has worked reliably. Students met with academic advisors to receive their access codes and could register at their leisure. In addition, the system allowed for continuous dropping and adding, which, although it lent itself to some abuses, made recordkeeping much easier.

Of course, the most important reason to encourage the growth of technology on campus was to enhance academics. While "chalk-and-talk" continued (and probably always will in this author's humble opinion) as the primary method of conveying instruction, technology allowed some students to learn in a different and a creative way. To the contemporary eye, some of the early initiatives seem anachronistic at best. Early discussions centered around providing computer labs across campus where students could draft papers and look for additional research materials on primitive search engines, never imaging the PC, the Mac, or the Internet. With the arrival of the Internet in 1994, uses for technology expanded. By the early twenty-first century, concerns about the campus network ended, as new wireless technology allowed students to use the campus technology even if they lived off campus. Some technology faded, like the WINGS electronic portfolio for students that proved very time-consuming to create. For the most part technology improved the university, and nothing made a greater difference than the laptop computer program.

As early as 1996, administrators began to think about the advantages of making WSU a "laptop university," one of the first in the nation. After consulting with experts who had initiated laptop projects on other campuses, President Krueger cautiously moved ahead with the initiative, which offered several bonuses. For one thing, laptops solved the problem of the ever-increasing demand for computer lab space on campus, since such facilities could eventually be phased out. Secondly, laptops seemed more egalitarian, allowing students living off campus to complete their work late in the evening. Finally, the laptop program generated money for the campus through student leases, enabling the university to hire technological gurus to maintain the equipment, advise faculty on use of computers, and serve students better. Despite the obvious advantages, the initiation of the program limped forward slowly, which allowed valuable time to work out problems. Could there, for example, be a single platform or did the university need to offer both PCs and Macs? When some disciplines argued for the Mac, the administration decided to accommodate both. Could students bring laptops from home and pay a fee for maintenance? This proved impractical, and eventually all students had to lease. Did all students have to lease laptops immediately, or could currently enrolled students (as of 1997) chose to exempt themselves? Laptops became mandatory in the year 2000. Although some disciplines and faculty members continued to be troglodytes, many jumped on the bandwagon. In scientific areas in particular, technology solved many instructional problems. And although some wished for simpler days, most agreed that technology had changed the university for the better in ways that nobody could have imagined twenty-five years ago.

Changing the Face of the Campus: The Beautification Program

Over the past twenty-five years, a number of achievements have allowed Winona State to stand out: its designation as one of the hundred "Best Buys" among colleges in the United States; its comprehensive technology initiatives; its improvements in student academic achievement; and various elements of the improved physical plant, most notably, the Residential College, the Krueger Library, and the new science building. At no time in its history had so much been done to improve the physical appearance of the campus. These years left behind the somewhat blighted urban arrangement with streets running through the middle of campus. By the turn of the century visiting alumni and prospective students alike praised the physical beauty of the grounds. Such attention to the surroundings seemed in keeping with the city's splendid location on Wapasha's prairie, tucked between the bluffs and the expanse of the blue Mississippi.

At the same time the Rochester campus moved wholesale to a modern location. A kind benefactor donated a large plot for the Rochester campus, providing plenty of parking for commuting students and room for future expansion, if necessary. No longer scattered haphazardly among the city's public buildings, the new location on the southeastern edge of the city allowed for enrollment growth. The Rochester campus now housed three separate entities: the local technical and community college, a branch of the University of Minnesota, and Winona State. Further, the new plant catered to the professional needs of the city, focusing on programs in nursing and computer technology. Meanwhile, Winona contented itself with remodeling, first dorms like Prentiss-Lucas, then Somsen Hall, then a space for daycare. President Thomas Stark revived Guy Maxwell's limited dream of an expanded football stadium, and later, under the impetus of Governor Perpich, got behind a new health and applied science building. But the 1980s were hard times for higher education, as the system as a whole struggled to maintain enrollment. Even with residence hall occupancy at over 100 percent, as we have seen, Stark was unable to win approval for a new, high-rise tower to be built beside Sheehan.

By the end of the 1980s, with President Krueger in place and with improving enrollment, optimism allowed for new capital projects. Not only did the legislature authorize the letting of bonds for what would become Stark Hall, but serious discussion emerged about Winona State's acquiring a West Campus. For years, the College of St. Teresa had been struggling to survive. The loss of accreditation proved a final blow, and in 1987, the college closed. What would happen to the beautiful facilities, which included several dormitories, a classroom building, a laboratory hall, a library, and several smaller buildings? Given WSU's growing enrollment, a number of visionaries advocated that the state should buy the entire campus for its relatively modest asking price, but the State University System bureaucrats balked. As a result, WSU rented a number of buildings in 1989, including two dormitories. Fortunately for the Winona community, instead of letting the campus fall into rack and ruin, the Hiawatha Foundation purchased it. Over time, Winona State purchased Lourdes Hall, a residence hall, and the Tau Center from the foundation, and negotiated agreements to use the sports facilities and rent other space. Lourdes Hall transformed itself into one of the university's exciting initiatives, the Residential College. Over the next fifteen years faculty developed themed courses, primarily in the liberal arts, to be delivered mostly to first-year students at Lourdes. Once renovated, the beautiful building also offered a magnificent dining hall and facilities where events like the World Music series and gamelon (a rare Indonesian instrument) concerts could take place.

After a struggle in the legislature, the university secured bonding for Stark Hall, the health science and engineering building that opened in the early 1990s. Boasting excellent laboratory facilities for both nursing and composite engineering, the building helped draw able students. Soon record numbers of students hoping to major in the competitive nursing program enrolled at the university, once more swelling the proportion of women. While composite engineering attracted much smaller numbers, its majors competed in exciting programs (like designing a light-weight automobile) and satisfied the growing need for plastic materials specialists. By the turn of the century, the fundamental sciences needed a new building with up-to-date laboratories in which to teach both basic courses and upper-division work in chemistry, biology, physics, and geoscience. Once again the entire campus rallied behind the project, and with the assistance of able local legislators Gene Pelowski, Steve Sviggum, and Bob Kierlin and a willing governor, Tim Pawlenty, the building came into fruition. In the fall of 2004, Dean Nancy Jannik proudly opened the new, as yet unnamed, facility for classes. Two years later, a remodeled Pasteur, now providing offices and basic classrooms, completed the science side of the campus.

Reinforcing its reputation as a primarily residential campus, WSU introduced its East Lake apartment complex in 2001. As part of the future, however, the campus master plan also offered the Gateway Center, a wholly new set of residence halls that would eventually replace the housing Quadrangle built in the 1960s. As such, this proposal fit in well with the campus beautification project, one of the most successful efforts of President Darrell Krueger's many years of service. In the 1990s, interior streets were removed from campus, allowing for green space and a series of fountains and gardens. With the removal of streets, parking moved to the exterior of campus, leaving faculty and commuters a short walk to offices and classroom buildings. The addition of a gazebo and an old clock donated by Norwest Bank made the center of campus especially attractive. On the periphery of campus some older buildings received facelifts and additions. New classrooms in Minné made current pedagogy more workable; Maxwell temporarily became a conference center and home to the budding wellness center; and Kryzko Commons added a solarium. At the same time, the campus infrastructure improved. Now the chiller loop extended all over campus, delivering air conditioning necessary in early fall, late spring, and summer and the even more important new boilers delivered warm air for the rest of the year. In the minds of many, Winona had become the most attractive campus in the MnSCU system and arguably outpaced many others around the country.

While dear to the heart of President Krueger, campus beautification required a team effort. Committees of faculty, staff, and students worked hard designing projects that would further academic and community efforts. Keeping in mind that these buildings had primarily an academic focus, faculty expressed their opinions about the way classrooms were configured and the types of equipment they contained. Understanding the need for a well-rounded experience, students advocated for a wellness center and better facilities for health, counseling, and placement. To make their out-of-class hours more palatable, the students argued for the need to upgrade the commons, and were among the strongest proponents for technology in classrooms, the library, and the residence halls. Maintenance did a wonderful job keeping the newer and remodeled buildings in peak condition, while the groundskeepers constructed greenhouses to start the flowers that bloomed for months (after all, it was Minnesota), planted ivy, and kept the green spaces clipped; the campus also contained at least one example of every species of tree native to Minnesota. With the beautification program came a campus with respect for the physical plant; pedestrians by and large kept to the sidewalks and litter became the exception rather than the rule. At no time since its founding had the campus looked so good.

The Future: The Past Meets the Present and the Future

As the university community approached the sesquicentennial and beyond, its leadership remained ambitious. The improvements undertaken since the dark days of the early 1980s had allowed people to dream. President Judith Ramaley and the faculty transformed the "new university" initiative into a more specific proposal called L-21. Based on Winona State's mission as a "community of learners improving our world," the L-21 project offered change and deeper learning. Restated simply, the plan was for students to learn differently, to work together differently, and to make a difference. Because WSU had become a learning-centered institution over the past twenty-five years, the entire university returned to Winona's original goal, when its founders created a normal school that would train much-needed teachers and serve the greater public good as a result of their work.

Putting the mission statement into action through the L-21 initiative will require the entire university's engagement and collaboration. Future generations must reflect upon their education and contend with an ever-changing global environment. Therefore, more academic experiences will be interdisciplinary and focused on problem solving. The new learning must incorporate technology, preparing students for the future. As an end result, students will be better prepared to participate in a democratic society; to understand and debate the issues of the day (the public good) and also to be fully prepared for the world of work (the private benefit). By teaching the entire community to gather evidence, reason analytically and debate civilly, meaningful change will result, continuing the path of advancement of recent decades.

"Enough of the abstractions and ideals," students (and others) shouted. "What do these concepts mean in a practical sense? How will they transform my life for the better?" Instead of the college years being a transitory and isolated experience, they will be integrated better into a person's entire life. Newly conceptualized first-year experience programs will soften the transition to university, while career development, encouraging student employment and internships, will make the exit a less wrenching experience. In between matriculation and graduation, integrated academic services where a student can ask about registration, financial aid, and related matters in a single location will free students from becoming captives of mind-numbing bureaucratic rules and regulations, at least if they act responsibly. While not rejecting traditional academic disciplines, the new scholarly opportunities will highlight more interdisciplinary engagement. For example, the Mississippi River Studies Center bonds together interdisciplinary academic interests with one of the primary assets of the community. More students will engage in active research projects with faculty sponsors. As a result, when the student graduates, he or she will be able to demonstrate to prospective employers the skills and attributes desired in the workforce. At the same time, as students participate in study abroad programs, travel study programs, internships or service learning experiences at remote sites, they will experience the transformative maturing moment that will make them good citizens in our contemporary society. Hopefully, these practical steps will convince the public that Winona State students have truly been involved in a productive and meaningful learning experience, and that Winona State is truly an engaged university.

A Return to Our Roots

Any lengthy voyage will likely subject a traveler to sudden storms and squalls, occasionally with near-fatal consequences. In its 150 years of existence, Winona State has weathered a number of heavy blows, but the recent period has seemed relatively quiescent. Perhaps the absence of serious problems resulted from the emphasis placed on preserving and valuing relationships, so that administration, faculty, staff, students, and community generally worked together for the common good. Perhaps calm resulted from a growing confidence in the university's mission, a mission that restored the emphasis on the public good that had provided the rationale for the founding of the institution a century and a half before. Having a common direction and goals has led to campus-wide agreement on the institution's future, an agreement that will extend beyond the sesquicentennial. Perhaps the quiescence resulted from the university's rededication to the five themes that made it great in the nineteenth century.

In other ways the past twenty-five years have recapitulated the institution's early origins. Back in the early days, the citizens of Winona provided a facility to house the normal school and made possible its very existence. With the addition of Stark Hall, Krueger Library, and the science lab facilities, the university can boast of a modern physical plant equal to any in the state. With the success of the campus beautification project, the university community can argue that the physical setting surpasses any other in the region. Like the pupils of the 1880s, today's students are largely residential, living in outstanding remodeled buildings like Lourdes Hall and the newly created East Lake apartments. And as in the 1860s and 1870s, the fact that most students live on or near campus helps to create a sense of community. Although in the past students have created occasional tensions with the city, recently the community and the students have made greater efforts to develop mutual understanding, respect, and academic partnership that benefit all. That is also the case in Rochester.

Above all else, Winona State University has regained its stature as an institution dedicated to academic excellence. A reinvigorated faculty and highly qualified students have made a real difference across the campus in recent years. The recent emphasis on educational quality is reminiscent of Winona's earlier years, when Principal Phelps and others brought the most modern pedagogy to this campus to serve as a model for the region and the nation. By selecting nationally known figures as Winona State University's last two presidents, the institution has regained its reputation as one that hires quality leaders. The results are obvious. Not only is Winona State among the leaders in terms of the use of technology for instructional purposes, but the campus's new traditions of assessing its successes and building on them are but two of the innovative developments of the past twenty-five years. Although the information age presents a whole new series of challenges for public higher education, WSU is well equipped to meet them. We are all stimulated by the prospects of returning to past values and demonstrating to the state and region that Winona State University will work for the public good, as it did in its historic past. The journey will be exciting.

Bibliography

Primary Sources

"Memories of WSTC," by Everett Edstrom. In Robert Dufresne, *Winona State University: A History of One Hundred Twenty-Five Years.* Winona: Winona State University, 1985.

"Reminiscent Sketches," by F. L. Cook, Clara Caswell Greening, Kate Berry Morey, E. A. Kirkpatrick, and David L. Kiehle. In Clyde O. Ruggles, *Historical Sketch and Notes: Winona State Normal School, 1860–1910.* Winona: Jones & Kroeger Co., 1910.

Videotaped interviews with Susan Day, Robert Dufresne, Joe Emanuel, Calvin Fremling, Roderick Henry, Ruth Hopf, Jacque Reidelberger, and Ken Wynia.

The Wenonah, 1911–1976.

The Winonan, 1922–2007.

The Winona Normal Bulletin, 1904–1919.

The Winona State College Bulletin, 1920–1960.

Secondary Sources

Curtiss-Wedge, Franklyn, ed. *The History of Winona County Minnesota*, 2 vols. Chicago: H. C. Cooper Jr. & Co., 1913.

Dufresne, Robert. *Winona State University: A History of One Hundred Twenty-Five Years*. Winona: Winona State University, 1985.

Ruggles, Clyde O. *Historical Sketch and Notes: Winona State Normal School, 1860–1910.* Winona: Jones & Kroeger Co., 1910.

Selle, Erwin S. *The Winona State Teachers' College: Historical Notes, 1910–1935*. Winona: Winona State Teachers' College, 1935.

Talbot, Jean. *First State Normal School 1860—Winona State College 1960*. Winona: Winona State College, 1960.

Index

F

G

H

I

J

K

L

M

N

About the Author

Peter Henderson, professor of history, began teaching at Winona State University in the autumn of 1989 after practicing law for eight years in Boston, Massachusetts. Since earning his PhD at the University of Nebraska–Lincoln, he has published several works on Latin American history. While at Winona State University, he has served as the dean of the College of Liberal Arts for five years and a single term as Faculty Association president. Over the years, he has collaborated with colleagues across campus on many committees, including of course the Sesquicentennial Celebration committee.

udy Abroad